AUSTRALIAN ENGLISH

Australian English

An Historical Study of the Vocabulary
1788-1898

W. S. RAMSON
Senior Lecturer in English
The Australian National University

AUSTRALIAN NATIONAL UNIVERSITY PRESS
CANBERRA

First published 1966

This book is copyright. Reproduction in whole or in part,
without permission, is forbidden.

Set in 11 point Linotype Baskerville on 12 point body with
18 point Baskerville italic headings and printed on double demy
96 lb Burnie English Finish paper by Halstead Press Pty Ltd, Sydney.

Registered in Australia for transmission by post as a book.

Foreword

Dr Ramson's book will satisfy a widely felt need for guidance on a subject that every Australian is interested in, the characteristics and the development of the Australian variation of the vocabulary of English. In the face of the impressionistic statements made about Australian English, the reader must often feel lost. He cannot believe that some of the comical distortions of language that are devised from time to time really represent the way a large number of Australians use the English language. He must wonder what evidence there might be to guide his judgment in the face of widespread unthinking acceptance of such extravagances.

He must find it hard to reconcile this kind of view with the claim that Australians have added a body of words of unusual colour and force to the language and that this stock of words is unusually extensive.

What are the sorts of words we have added? Can they be classified? How far are they a reflection of characteristic features of Australian life? How large is their number? Whence are they derived? How many can be claimed as genuine Australian inventions?

The answers to such questions that are dictated by a critical examination of evidence will surprise many. The claim so often made for the Australian that he has been uncommonly inventive in language has to be abandoned. The picture commonly painted of the Australian using a heavy proportion of slang terms in his talk when compared with speakers in other countries is difficult to justify by the evidence.

There is a folklore about Australian English which can readily be exploited in fiction or by the self-styled authoritative writer. Serious attempts to gather evidence and to interpret it critically go back a long way in

v

Australian history, as Dr Ramson's introductory chapter shows. Much of it has been done with great care and under difficulties. Heavy reliance had to be placed on the testimony of correspondents and on evidence of very doubtful authenticity, such as novels and short stories. There was hardly any opportunity to check the reliability of such testimony and there was always the certainty that a great amount of the material remained unrevealed.

Dr Ramson's research was done at a time when it was possible to take recorded spoken materials into account as well as printed materials and when financial assistance from the University of Sydney made it possible to use the technique of the questionnaire and gather evidence more widely and with a more clearly defined aim. His work is in the tradition of strict methods of scholarship. Many of us hope that we can now see the beginning of a time when financial support from research funds will make possible the organization of a team programme to gather and classify materials. Australian scholars will then be able increasingly to reveal to us the characteristics and the development of the Australian variant of English.

In the meantime, Dr Ramson's book is the best outline of our present knowledge of the subject available. It is to be hoped that the book will be widely read both for its own interest and for its demonstration that the subject deserves and rewards disciplined scientific investigation.

A. G. Mitchell

January 1966

Acknowledgments

THIS BOOK is based on material collected for a doctoral thesis submitted at the University of Sydney in 1961. I should like to thank first of all Professor A. G. Mitchell, who supervised the preparation of that thesis, for his inspiration, guidance, and help. I should like to thank also many other colleagues with whom I have discussed parts of this book: in particular, in Sydney, the members of the Australian Language Research Centre; in Oxford, Mr R. W. Burchfield; and in Canberra, Professor A. D. Hope, Professor G. H. Russell, and Mr G. K. W. Johnston, Professor C. M. H. Clark, Professor K. S. Inglis, and Mr D. W. A. Baker.

My thanks are due also to the librarians of the School of General Studies Library and the National Library of Australia; of the Fisher and Mitchell Libraries in Sydney; of the British Museum and the Royal Commonwealth Society in London, and of Rhodes House, Oxford; also to the archivists of the Church Missionary Society, the London Missionary Society, the Methodist Missionary Society, the Society of Friends, and the Society for the Propagation of the Gospel, all in London.

I am indebted also to the major historians of British, American, and Australian English, and have drawn heavily on the *Oxford English Dictionary*, the *English Dialect Dictionary*, M. M. Mathews's *Dictionary of Americanisms*, Edward Morris's *Austral English*, A. G. Mitchell's *Supplement* to *Chambers's Shorter English Dictionary*, and the writings of S. J. Baker. Some of the material in this book has already been published in *Australian Literary Studies*, the *Australian Quarterly*, *Southerly*, and a Commonwealth Literary Fund lecture published by the Australian National University. I am grateful to the editors for permission to use this again.

My thanks are due also to the British Council, for a grant which enabled me to study in London in 1958-9, and to the University of Sydney and the Australian National University for their help. I would like finally to express my thanks to Margaret Hamilton, who typed the manuscript and helped with the checking, and to the editorial department of the Australian National University Press, for their patience and help.

W. S. RAMSON

Australian National University
November 1965

Contents

1

The Place of Australian English

THIS ACCOUNT of the vocabulary of Australian English covers a period of 110 years, a period that begins with the founding of the first settlement in New South Wales in 1788 and ends, just before the turn of the century, with the publication in 1898 of the only historical dictionary of the English language in Australia. This is not a long time in the history of a language, but it is long enough for certain distinctive features of the Australian vocabulary to have emerged, for the general make-up of the vocabulary to have become apparent, and for a pronunciation, relatively uniform and individual, to have developed. And, if further evidence of maturity is wanted, it is long enough for a 'literary' Australian English to have been adopted, originally by the *Bulletin* school of short-story writers.

At the end of the nineteenth century the linguistic situation was much simpler than it is now, when new influences on the vocabulary have to be taken into account. The slang of Australians serving overseas, based on that in use in Australian cities or in the countryside, has mingled, borrowing and being borrowed, with the slang of other servicemen, British, American, and European. Servicemen from other countries, notably from the United States, have visited Australia. What is more, improved communications between the different English-speaking countries have given greater opportunities for borrowing from one dialect to another, extending and enriching the vocabulary that is common to them all. Linguistically the situation of Australian English in the twentieth century is more complex and heterogeneous than it was in the nineteenth century.

1

Early American English, similarly, was more of an entity than contemporary American English. Noah Webster had been convinced, in 1789, that the isolation of the United States from England and the rest of Europe would lead to the emergence of a new language in the New World; that there would be 'in a course of time, a language in North America, as different from the future language of England, as the modern Dutch, Danish and Swedish are from the German, or from one another'.[1] Webster looked back over a period of almost 200 years in which English had been spoken in the United States in relative isolation, a period in which certain trends had already emerged and the language developed an individual character. Edward Morris, in 1898, looked back over a shorter but essentially similar period in the development of Australian English. And there were undoubtedly many Australians, at the end of the nineteenth century, who felt that the fostering and maintenance of an identifiably Australian vocabulary and pronunciation were essential to their growing sense of identity and national pride.

By the end of the nineteenth century, the vocabulary and pronunciation of Australian English had become distinctively different from any model which British English could supply. There has always been disagreement about the status of the new dialect, about the extent to which it had acquired a character of its own, distinctively Australian and indicative of characteristics which were not simply linguistic but part of the Australian ethos. The example of American English is again instructive. In particular, a knowledge of the attitudes adopted by historians of American English may help us to assess the interpretations which some historians of Australian English have placed on their material.

Noah Webster, for instance, championing the Americans' use of English and looking on British English with the passionate contempt of a reformer, argued that the Americans should not seek uniformity with a corrupt and

[1] As quoted in G. P. Krapp, *The English Language in America*, vol. 1, p. 9.

steadily deteriorating British English but should deliberately strive to establish a vocabulary and usage which would gain stature as their nation itself grew. As he wrote in his *Grammatical Institute*, in 1783:

The author wishes to promote the honour and prosperity of the confederated republics of America and chearfully throws his mite into the common treasure of patriotic exertions. This country must in some future time, be as distinguished by the superiority of her literary improvements, as she is already by the liberality of her civil and ecclesiastical constitutions. Europe is grown old in folly, corruption and tyranny—in that country laws are perverted, manners are licentious, literature is declining and human nature debased. For America in her infancy to adopt the present maxims of the old world, would be to stamp the wrinkles of decrepid age upon the bloom of youth and to plant the seeds of decay in a vigorous constitution.[2]

Almost 150 years later, in the decade following World War I, similarly nationalistic views (less strongly held since the need for justification no longer existed) were expressed by H. L. Mencken in *The American Language*. Mencken's views were based on an examination of the spoken rather than the written language. Aware of an extensive colloquial and slang vocabulary in which the differences between British and American English were vast, he argued that 'the American form of the English language was plainly departing from the parent stem', and that 'it seemed at least likely that the differences between American and English would go on increasing'.[3] Standard English, he wrote,

has been arrested in its growth by its purists and grammarians, and burdened with irrational affectations by fashionable pretension. It shows no living change since the reign of Samuel Johnson. Its tendency is to combat

[2] *Grammatical Institute*, pt 1, p. 14; as quoted in Krapp, *The English Language in America*, vol. 1, p. 8.
[3] H. L. Mencken, *The American Language* (4th ed.), p. vi. Mencken describes this as the view he argued in the first three editions. It is slightly modified in the fourth.

all that expansive gusto which made for its pliancy and resilience in the days of Shakespeare. In place of the old loose-footedness there is set up a preciosity which, in one direction, takes the form of clumsy artificialities in the spoken language, and in another shows itself in the even clumsier Johnsonese of so much current English writing—the Jargon denounced by Sir Arthur Quiller-Couch in his Cambridge lectures. . . .

Let American confront a novel problem alongside English, and immediately its superior imaginativeness and resourcefulness become obvious. *Movie* is better than *cinema*; and the English begin to admit the fact by adopting the word; it is not only better American, it is better English. *Billboard* is better than *hoarding*. *Officeholder* is more honest, more picturesque, more thoroughly Anglo-Saxon than *public-servant*. *Stemwinder* somehow has more life in it, more fancy and vividness, than the literal *keyless-watch*. Turn to the terminology of *railroading* (itself, by the way, an Americanism): its creation fell upon the two peoples equally, but they tackled the job independently. The English, seeking a figure to denominate the wedge-shaped fender in front of a locomotive, called it a *plough*; the Americans, characteristically, gave it the far more pungent name of *cow-catcher*. So with the casting which guides the wheels from one rail to another. The English called it a *crossing-plate*; the Americans, more responsive to the suggestion in its shape, called it a *frog*. American is full of what Bret Harte called the 'saber-cuts of Saxon'; it meets Montaigne's ideal of 'a succulent and nervous speech, short and compact, not as much delicate and combed out as vehement and brusque, rather arbitrary than monotonous, not pedantic but soldierly, as Suetonius called Caesar's Latin'. One pictures the common materials of English dumped into a pot, exotic flavorings added, and the bubblings assiduously and expectantly skimmed. What is old and respected is already in decay the moment it comes into contact with what is new and vivid. 'When we Americans are through with the English language,' says Mr Dooley, 'it will look as if it had been run over by a musical comedy.'[4]

4 Ibid., pp. 93-4, 95-6.

Opposed to Mencken's *American Language,* in method and content, was Krapp's *English Language in America,* published six years later than the first edition of Mencken. And it is, as Albert Marckwardt has argued, 'by no means overstraining a point to maintain that the difference in these two titles reflects a thoroughgoing difference in attitude toward the material under consideration'.[5] Whereas Mencken had sought to indicate the individuality and vitality of American English, Krapp, working mostly from written sources, stressed the links between British and American English, and treated American not as a 'new language' but as a branch of British English which would be understood the more readily for being studied in relation to it.

The major historians of Australian English have adopted one or other of these positions. E. E. Morris saw his task as the recording of 'Austral English', the recording of the new words and the new uses of old words added to the English language by settlers in Australia and New Zealand.[6] Professor A. G. Mitchell, stressing that Australian English must be seen in its proper relation to British English, has deplored the promulgation of the idea that 'the spirit of a young nation may be judged by the number of colourful colloquialisms and idioms that are developed in its language'. With both pronunciation and vocabulary in mind, he has argued that 'it is foolish to see a virtue in the mere fact of difference and to accept the implication that the greater the difference the better'.[7]

At the opposite pole is Sidney J. Baker, whose main work, *The Australian Language,* was published in 1945. Neither in method nor achievement does Baker's work stand comparison with Mencken's, yet his position is essentially the same. He has adapted Mencken's title to his own work; and it is clear that, like Mencken, he has accepted the implications of that title. He is not concerned

---

[5] *American English,* p. 4.

[6] *Austral English: A Dictionary of Australasian Words, Phrases and Usages,* p. xi.

[7] 'Australian English', *Australian Quarterly* (March 1951), vol. xxiii, no. 1, pp. 15, 10.

with Australian English as one of several dialects which could profitably be studied in relation to British English; and he does not accept the view that the historical and comparative study of Australian and British English would show the two in a far closer relation than is usually thought to exist. His approach is rather to accentuate the differences, to see Australian English as something new and unique, which has severed its connections with the mother-tongue and which has, from the first, developed along lines peculiar to itself.

He is led, therefore, just as Mencken was, to reject the traditional English criticisms. Those features which English critics had noted as divergences from the polite norm of Standard English Baker takes as characteristics of 'the new language'.[8] What were lapses of taste or convention become signs of originality and inventiveness. 'It is', he writes, 'as though the Australian felt that the English of England were inadequate or effete, and had deliberately set himself the task of revivifying it and adding colour and virility to it.'[9]

Australian English is younger than American, its history less complex; so that Baker's position is open to even more criticism than Mencken's. There has been no Australian Declaration of Independence nor, despite those exuberantly patriotic writers who have sought to emphasize the distinctiveness of their language, has Australian English moved as far from British English as American had in the corresponding period; and there is now little likelihood of a continued drift away from British English.

The greater part of the Australian's vocabulary is still Standard English: the *Concise Oxford Dictionary* serves the Australian almost as well as it serves the Englishman and, in many areas of usage, he has no occasion to depart from the established British English pattern. In slang, in the colloquial vocabulary, in various occupational vocabularies, and, most extensively of all, in the nomenclature of indigenous flora and fauna, there are differences. And

[8] *The Australian Language*, p. 3.
[9] *Australia Speaks*, p. 13.

many of these new words—or new uses of old words—
have drawn distinctively Australian connotations from
the context in which they are most commonly found. But
to take these, to take particularly those differences that
arise in slang, the least permanent and least well-recorded
section of the vocabulary, and dignify them with the term
language is to offer a seriously distorted view of the character of Australian English. It is easy enough to compile
lists of slang words, but notoriously difficult to ascertain
their currency and derivation; one does not have to look
far for examples of words which are thought of as Australian and used to illustrate national characteristics of the
Australian, but which are either widely current in British
or American slang or, at the other extreme, nonce words
or words with a small and local currency embalmed in the
collection of some over-enthusiastic lexicographer.

What sort of words, then, make up Australian English?
No one in his right mind would want to rewrite the
Oxford English Dictionary, duplicating as much of its
material as has a history of usage in standard Australian.
For all practical purposes, Australian English consists of
the additions to British English. These additions may take
several forms: they may be words completely new to
English, words borrowed from the Aborigines or coined
by the colonists; they may be words new to British English
but current in and borrowed from other branches of
English, notably American; they may be words familiar
to the speakers of British English which, in Australia,
have been put to different uses; or words, unfamiliar perhaps to the speakers of Standard British English, with
long histories of use in less refined circles, in the slang of
the lower classes or in regional dialect vocabularies.

A vocabulary of this sort, maintaining the basic stock
of the British English vocabulary and used by people who
are almost exclusively of British descent, can only be
profitably examined if its relation to British English is
kept constantly in mind. Its character will be derived not
only from the number and nature of the additions but
from the number and nature of the British English words
put to different uses, and of the slang or dialect words

B

that survive and are perhaps brought into more general currency.

This is, most emphatically, not the character of a new language. The vocabulary is being expanded, it is true, but by exactly the same means as the vocabulary of nineteenth-century British English, and by the same means, but on a much smaller scale, as American English. The differences are not as great as in American English and they do not seem to me to be growing in importance, whereas Mencken, in his fourth edition, can argue that American English is no longer simply developing in a different way from British English but is now actually in terms of vigour, inventiveness, and numerical strength, leading British English away from its traditional path.[10]

The material in this book is arranged not chronologically but, rather, in such a way as to indicate the main sources from which the vocabulary of the settlers was expanded. Thus in chapter 4 are discussed regional dialect and slang words which were not current in Standard English but have become a part of Australian English; in chapter 5 words which have changed their meanings in Australia or, by the processes of composition or derivation, been formed into new words. In chapters 6 and 7 borrowings from Aboriginal languages are discussed, as well as borrowings from American English, the only branch of English which has influenced Australian English at all extensively. Finally, in chapter 8, some explanation is offered of the smallness of the influence which the vocabularies of immigrant minorities have had on Australian English, a smallness in sharp contrast to the extensive and varied nature of their contribution to American English.

Chapters 2 and 3 are essential to the thesis of this book, but the reader who is interested primarily in the words which go to make up the vocabulary of Australian English may prefer to pass them over and perhaps return at leisure. The study of Australian English is in its infancy. Pioneer explorations like those of Morris and Baker

[10] *The American Language* (4th ed.), p. vi.

derive importance not only from the material they have collected but from the points of view they have expressed and propagated. Baker's thesis, refined and greatly extended in currency by Eric Partridge, has become widely adopted, and many Australians think of their vocabulary, as they think of their accent, as being distinctively Australian and markedly different from that of British English.

For this reason I have sought, in chapter 2, to assess the contribution of all previous writers on the subject of Australian English and to show how, just as in the United States, differing points of view have become entrenched in the literature of the subject and sometimes stand in the way of a fresh and unbiased assessment of the evidence. Much of this material has been published in this century and some of it takes account only of contemporary developments in the vocabulary: its importance to this study results not from the commentary it offers but from the contribution it makes towards the definition of the established attitudes to Australian English. In chapter 3 I have surveyed the classes of written source material from which evidence can most profitably be collected and have argued against the uncritical acceptance of evidence which abounds in certain classes of material but which may give an altogether misleading impression of the currency of some words and of the character of the vocabulary generally.

It is perhaps unnecessary to add that this book is not intended to be a comprehensive account of the Australian vocabulary in the nineteenth century. The days of the one-man dictionary are over: I hope only to give some indication of the composition of Australian English before the turn of the century and of the areas of the vocabulary which would most repay further study.

2

Earlier Studies of the Australian Vocabulary

IN 1898 two dictionaries of Australian English were published. One, E. E. Morris's *Austral English*, deficient in many respects and dated as it is, remains the only historical dictionary of Australian English. The other, Joshua Lake's Australasian supplement to *Webster's International Dictionary*, has long since been incorporated into the body of *Webster's*. Their publication towards the end of the nineties marks the period in which Australian words and idioms first acquired a general literary currency and climaxes the most productive period of investigation into the history of Australian English. With the exception of Sidney J. Baker's forays in the forties and fifties, and the activities of the newly formed Australian Language Research Centre, the present century has so far produced no fresh attempt at a sustained and fruitful investigation of evidence drawn from primary sources.

The dictionaries of Morris and Lake were preceded by a handful of slang dictionaries which, with one exception, date from the closing decades of the nineteenth century. The exception is James Hardy Vaux's *New and Comprehensive Vocabulary of the Flash Language*, compiled by Vaux at Newcastle, New South Wales, in 1812 and published with his *Memoirs* in 1819. Quite apart from being the first, Vaux was the most unlikely of Australian lexicographers. A ne'er-do-well, three times transported to New South Wales for picking pockets and other petty thefts, he was nonetheless a cut above his fellows and sufficiently well-educated to observe their habits dispassionately. Vaux presented his *Vocabulary of the Flash Language* to Thomas Skottowe, the commandant at Newcastle, trusting that it would afford him some amusement from its novelty and that, from the correctness of its definitions, he would occasionally find it useful in his magisterial capacity[1]—a not altogether impractical object when we remember that Tench had commented in 1793 on the need for an interpreter in courts of law.[2]

The *Vocabulary* is not, and was never intended to be, a record of the English in use during the early years of the colony. There are, for instance, no words of Aboriginal origin and no words with a specifically Australian reference, though Vaux could, had he wished, have compiled quite an extensive list of both these classes, even as early as 1812. The restricted nature of the *Vocabulary* is further indicated by the apology, which Vaux apparently felt bound to offer in his dedication to Thomas Skottowe:

> however the theme may be condemned as exceptionable by narrow minds [he wrote] I feel confident you possess too much liberality of sentiment to reject its writer as utterly depraved, because he has acquired an extensive knowledge on a subject so obviously disgraceful. True it is, that in the course of a chequered and eventful life, I have intermixed with the most dissolute and unprincipled characters, and that a natural quickness of conception, and most retentive memory, have rendered me familiar with their language and system of operations.[3]

Vaux's was a vocabulary of English criminal cant, some but by no means all of which was used in convict circles in New South Wales. It is significant that, although a number of the words he records can be found in use during the 1840s, they have remained cant and have not become an acceptable part of the colonial vocabulary. In Alexander Harris's *Settlers and Convicts* (1847), and par-

[1] *Vocabulary of the Flash Language*, Dedication. The *Vocabulary* has recently been made accessible in N. McLachlan's edition of the *Memoirs*.

[2] W. Tench, *Complete Account of the Settlement at Port Jackson in New South Wales*, p. 207.

[3] Vaux, loc. cit.

ticularly in his novel, *The Emigrant Family* (1849), some of these words are used, mostly in the speech of convicts or ex-convicts and with the obvious intention of distinguishing this from the speech of other settlers. Harris uses, for example, *blunt* and *brads*, both meaning 'money'; *cross*, used of illegal and dishonest practices (the opposite being *square*); *dab*, 'bed', the place where one *dabs it up*; *family*, the whole fraternity of thieves and others who get their living *on the cross* being known as *the family*; *flat*, 'honest man or square cove' (the opposite being a *sharp*, or *cross cove*); *plant*, as a verb meaning 'to hide', or a noun, 'the place of concealment'; and *trap*, 'a policeman'.

By Harris's time there had of course been changes. The old terms had been adapted to the new environment, *the family* were no longer pickpockets but had become cattle-thieves, their activities *on the cross* included cattle-stealing and rebranding, their *plant* was a herd of cattle tucked away in the back part of a run. A few words recorded by Vaux had moved up a little to become general slang: *cove*, by which Vaux understood 'the master of a house or shop', was used of the boss of a station; *gammon*, 'flattery, deceit or pretence', was used widely, particularly in Aboriginal pidgin; *new chum* and *old chum*, used originally of fellow convicts, gained a wider currency; and *swag*, recorded by Vaux as stolen 'wearing-apparel, linen, or piece-goods', as opposed to plate or jewellery, was used by Harris in its present sense, 'a bundle of personal belongings'.

Vaux, according to Sidney J. Baker, provides 'a fairly accurate picture of the type of language used in Australia during the first decade or so of last century',[4] but this is clearly not so. The *Vocabulary* is made up of words which were used by one section of the community only, and the fact that some of these words, recorded by Vaux in 1812, were still in use in the forties is evidence not of the vitality of Australian slang, but of the continued use in the colony of certain types of English slang. To look to Vaux, as Baker does, for an indication of the language in use in

[4] *The Australian Language*, p. 25.

the colony at that time, or even for 'a pointer for the way our language was to go',[5] is to place a wrong emphasis on what is, within its own terms of reference, a competently recorded and valuable glossary.

Vaux's *Memoirs* achieved sufficient notoriety to run into three editions, but the *Vocabulary*, which accompanied only the first of these, was quickly forgotten and no further attempt was made to record words in use in Australia until towards the end of the century, when several dictionaries, mostly of slang, were published. Some of these sounded a great deal more exciting than they in fact were. The anonymous *Sydney Slang Dictionary* (1882?) comprising 'All The Slang Words and Phrases in Use in Sydney and in The Shadows of Life', is a very short vocabulary purporting to record vulgarisms current in Sydney in the 1880s. Very few of the words are Australian and the dictionary is useful only in so far as it provides some evidence of the early currency of a small number of words. *Bludger*, for instance, is defined in its original Australian sense as 'a plunderer in company with a prostitute', and a few other words like *dart, lamb down, shicer,* and *wallaby track* are recorded. On the whole, however, the *Sydney Slang Dictionary* is little more than misleading, not only because of its omission of established Australianisms but also because of its inclusion of words which were almost certainly never used in Australia. The dictionary records, for instance, *Haymarket Hectors*, 'Bullies who, in the interests of prostitutes, infect the neighbourhood of Leicester Square and the Haymarket', and *pec*, 'Eton for money, from Latin PECUNIA'.

Cornelius Crowe's *Australian Slang Dictionary*, published in 1895, is a more extensive collection of words than either of these two earlier dictionaries. Crowe addresses his work to 'police and public' and, in his preface, claims to have recorded the slang of different occupational and social groups in the city, adding that few of the terms the dictionary contains

have been invented by the Australian criminals; the

most of them have been brought into use by the criminal classes who have emigrated here from different parts of the world where criminals have had almost a language of their own for centuries past.

Much of the interest of Crowe's work comes from his inclusion of words which are not properly within the scope of a slang dictionary, words like *backblocks, buckjumper, bushranger, jackeroo*, and the goldmining terms *to dolly* and *to fossick*, and from the number of bush idioms which are recorded for the first time in a dictionary published in Australia and clearly intended for the lay reader.

A reviewer in the *Bulletin* commented that many of the words listed by Crowe were 'either not Australian or not slang',[6] and this question of the status in English of a number of words well established in Australia seems also to have troubled Karl Lentzner, whose *Dictionary of the Slang-English of Australia and of Some Mixed Languages* was published three years earlier.[7] In his preface Lentzner makes the point that many of the words of 'the rich and racy Slang of the fifth continent' were 'invented because they were absolutely needed, or because they expressed some idea more ingeniously, sententiously, and amusingly than others had done'; he suggests that these words made necessary by the new environment are not properly slang, but is uncertain also of their relationship to the 'Queen's English'. In fact, Australian English does not seem to have been regarded by any of its collectors as an independent and respectable branch of English until the publication of dictionaries by Morris and Lake in 1898.

[6] 17 August 1895; quoted by Baker, *The Australian Language*, p. 27.

[7] There is a short article by Lentzner, 'Australisches Englisch', in *Englische Studien*, vol. xi (1888), pp. 173-4, in which three quotations on the 'purity' of Australian English pronunciation are introduced from J. A. Froude's *Oceana or England and her Colonies* and supported from Lentzner's own observations. Lentzner's dictionary was reviewed by W. Sattler, *Englische Studien*, vol. xvi (1892), p. 416. Other signs of the growing interest in Australian English are a short article in *Taalstudie*, vol. 9 (1888) by C. Ehrensperger, and an unsigned vocabulary in *All the Year Round*, 30 July 1887, pp. 64-8.

Lentzner's dictionary is an extraordinary compilation and is divided into sections, the largest of which is a vocabulary of 'Australian and Bush Slang'. There are shorter vocabularies of Anglo-Indian, West Indian and South African slang and of Chinese pidgin, followed by a lengthy appendix in which extracts from articles relevant to the vocabularies are reprinted.[8] Though Lentzner's vocabulary of Australian English is the first to use quotations, both to illustrate a word's use and to give evidence of its currency, it is of little value beside the dictionaries of Morris and Lake. None of the quotations is properly identified, dates, page numbers and bibliographical data being omitted. Usually Lentzner gives the author's name and the title of the book, sometimes only the author's name. For a number of quotations from newspapers, only the name of the newspaper is given.

It is doubtful if more than half the words recorded are in fact Australian. Lentzner draws heavily on Vaux's *Memoirs* for evidence of the use of words like *Alderman Lushington*, 'intoxicating drink'; *to back-slang*, 'to enter stealthily'; *a back slum*, 'a back room'; *bands*, 'hunger'; *burick*, 'a whore'; *buz-cove*, 'a pickpocket'; *to gammon*, 'deceive'; and *to put a down upon a man*, 'to inform against him'. There is no evidence that these words were generally current or that their Australian use differed from the English. A number of general English and American slang words are recorded, American borrowings usually being indicated.

Lentzner's coverage of bush idiom is much fuller than Crowe's but is to some extent invalidated by his almost complete dependence on the works of D. B. W. Sladen, on A. C. Grant's *Bush Life in Queensland* (1881), and W. Finch-Hatton's *Advance Australia* (1885). These are literary sources and none is early enough to be of much use in tracing the early history of the words recorded. It is

[8] These include a note on Australian English from R. E. N. Twopeny's *Town Life in Australia*, pp. 243-6, and specimens of Australian and Melanesian pidgin from articles by H. Schuchardt, *Englische Studien*, vol. xii, pp. 470-4; and vol. xiii, pp. 158-62.

therefore for its curiosity value more than its usefulness that Lentzner's dictionary remains interesting, though it is sometimes useful to have his frequently discursive comments on words, particularly those omitted by Morris.

Despite some obvious weaknesses the dictionaries compiled by Morris and Lake in 1898 are indispensable to the historical study of Australian English. Morris first applied consistently the historical principles of the *Oxford English Dictionary*, seeking not simply to provide a list of words and meanings but to establish through the use of illustrative quotations the development and range of each word's meaning; Lake, in his supplement to *Webster's Dictionary*, usefully complemented Morris's historical treatment by giving an apparently accurate and balanced picture of Australian English in the nineties. Both men were for a time on the staff of Melbourne Grammar, Morris as headmaster from 1875 until 1883, when he was appointed Professor of English, French, and German Languages at the University of Melbourne, and Lake as an assistant master. As lexicographers, both were amateurs, though Lake, whose *Supplement* was prepared under the supervision of G. L. Kittredge, was later appointed to the staff of *Webster's Dictionary*.

Whereas Lentzner had been so uncertain of the character of the vocabulary he was recording as to be unable to establish clearly its relationship either to slang or to Standard English, Morris and Lake carefully distinguished a number of classes of words which made up the Australian vocabulary as they saw it. Lake, using a more rigid classification than Morris, distinguished five main classes: native borrowings; 'new words or phrases formed by the colonists on the basis of English words already existing'; provincial words 'which have gained a wider currency from their adoption into colonial use'; scientific names in general use; and 'English words and phrases which have acquired a sense in the colonies differing more or less from that which they bear in England'.[9]

Morris's classification is not significantly different

9 Preface to the *Supplement*.

though, by a little somewhat unscientific subdivision, he achieves a total of nine classes of words: English names of flora and fauna applied to Australian species because of some real or fancied resemblance between the two; English words whose meanings have been extended; native borrowings with extended meanings; anglicizations of native words; 'fanciful, picturesque, or humorous' names given to flora and fauna; coinages 'arising from quite new objects or orders of things'; scientific names which are exclusively Australian; and slang 'of which the element [recorded] is comparatively small'.[10] The differences between the two classifications are not as important as the recognition of a new branch of English, what Morris called 'Austral English' and defined as

> all the new words and the new uses of old words that have been added to the English language by reason of the fact that those who speak English have taken up their abode in Australia, Tasmania and New Zealand.[11]

Australian English had, if a little belatedly, come of age.

Morris, perhaps following too literally the *Oxford English Dictionary* policy of giving space to scientific words which are English in form rather than to slang words, attaches a greater importance to the nomenclature of flora and fauna than Lake; many words for the use of which there is little evidence are included and the impression of Australian English given by the dictionary is unbalanced. This lack of balance was commented on in contemporary reviews, critics for several Australian newspapers deploring the inclusion of little-used words at the expense of more widely used slang words and phrases.[12] A. E. H. Swaen,

[10] *Austral English*, pp. xvi-xvii.
[11] Ibid., p. xi.
[12] See, e.g. *Bulletin*, 18 December 1897 (Red Page); *Australasian*, 22 January 1898, p. 217; *Sydney Morning Herald*, 1 January 1898. The *Bulletin* review, attributed by Baker (*Australian Language*, p. 31n.) to A. G. Stephens, makes an unpleasant personal attack on Morris and then, without taking into account the difficulties of compiling the dictionary, details a number of weaknesses.

reviewing the dictionary in *Englische Studien*,[13] accepted the lack of balance as characteristic of Australian English at that stage of its development. Lake's vocabulary, prepared for a general American dictionary and subject to its editorial policy, has no excesses of this sort.[14]

The most important feature of Morris's dictionary is its citing of quotations to illustrate the use and where possible the development of words and meanings peculiar to Australian English. In doing this Morris followed the practice of the editors of the *Oxford English Dictionary* (who were able to call on a large number of voluntary readers), and some of the weaknesses of his dictionary are a result of the size of the task he undertook with little help or experience and with no earlier Australian dictionary to serve as a guide. There is little difficulty now in finding quotations which are in many instances earlier than those given by Morris, or in supplying accurate derivations for words, particularly those of American or English dialect origin. Lake uses quotations only to illustrate the meaning and application of a word; he does not record early occurrences and in many instances omits the source and date of the quotation. Thus, although the *Supplement* has a balanced and reasonably comprehensive selection of Australian words current in the 1890s, with meanings well defined and illustrated, it is of less value to the historical study of Australian English than is Morris's dictionary, unselective and inaccurate as this often is.

It is clear from his preface that in collecting quotations

---

[13] Vol. xxvi, pp. 111-12. There is a descriptive review, 'Austral English and Slang', by H. A. Strong in *University Extension Journal*, vol. 3, no. 23, pp. 70-1. Professor Strong describes the dictionary, comments on a number of Morris's derivations, and concludes a short note on Australian pronunciation with the judgment that 'the London dialect [i.e. Cockney] is that which of any comes nearest to the common dialect of Australia'. This review is noted by E. Nader, *Englische Studien*, vol. xxix, p. 462.

[14] Interestingly enough Morris, in his Preface, acknowledges his debt to Lake, 'the friend who has given me most help of all', for subediting the names of flora and fauna and contributing much of the material in these sections.

for the dictionary, Morris relied greatly on correspondents. Some of these were specialists in their respective fields and some were casual readers who sent in quotations in response to requests for assistance published in a number of newspapers. Checking quotations received in this way is burdensome, and it is possible that a number of minor inaccuracies, especially in dating, result from this. More important is the inclusion of· non-lexicographical material,[15] words which were not widely used,[16] and etymologies, of Aboriginal words particularly, for which there is no clear evidence.[17]

The publication of Morris's dictionary led to an increased interest in Australian words and several vocabularies, mainly of slang words, were compiled in the early years of the present century.[18] Between 1900 and 1910 S. E. O'Brien and A. G. Stephens gathered their Material for a Dictionary of Australian Slang.[19] This is little more than a collection of notes, but it is hard to see how the completed dictionary could have been of any value. The selection of words is careless: American and English slang words, obsolescent and localized expressions and abbrevi-

[15] See the entries for *billy, Botany Bay, kangaroo, larrikin, wombat.*

[16] The *Bulletin* reviewer (23 April 1898) notes *skullbanker, Jack the Painter, coast, countmuster, rage,* and *scrubdangler* as obsolescent words used only in parts of Victoria.

[17] See the entries for *budgerigar, billabong, corella, pituri.*

[18] See, e.g. J. Hight, *Manual of Derivation and Composition of Words* (n.d.; Baker suggests 1906), which briefly summarizes Morris's introduction. There is a useful essay by Nettie Palmer, 'Austral English', in *Talking it Over,* pp. 38-43, which discusses some of the shortcomings of Morris's dictionary. Joseph Wright's *The English Dialect Dictionary* records a number of dialect words used in Australia. Wright's information is taken from Morris and from a number of contemporary Australian novels and descriptions of life in Australia. A number of Australian slang words are recorded by J. S. Farmer and W. E. Henley in a *Dictionary of Slang and Colloquial English.* Some of their datings are taken from Morris. See also the Australasian edition of *The World's Standard Dictionary* revised by C. M. Stevans and published in Auckland in 1915, which has a supplement of Australasian words, mainly colloquial and drawn largely from Morris and Lake.

[19] Typescript, Mitchell Library, Sydney.

ated place-names are included with no reference to their origin or currency, as are a number of Australian words, for example *assigned, blacktracker, boomerang,* and *bora,* which have never been slang; definitions, where provided, are frequently only rather lengthy comments on a word's use and supposed etymology. There is no attempt to illustrate the use of words with quotations.

The interest in Australian English which Morris's dictionary stirred up is perhaps even more clearly indicated by the number of letters which poured into the *Bulletin* around the turn of the century and by the publication of the first of a number of articles which examined the material collected by Morris and Lake and sought out trends or characteristic features of Australian English. Two of these, concerned particularly with the origins of words, were published in 1908. 'A.W.G.', writing in the *Lone Hand* of November 1908, followed Lake in suggesting an English provincial origin for many words commonly regarded as Australian, and stressed the smallness of the number of Aboriginal words which were not zoological or botanical names or words relating to features of Aboriginal life.[20] And J. W. Garth, writing in the *Australian Magazine* of the same month (pp. 1249-52), commented on the number of generally used slang words and phrases which could be traced back to mining slang, examining the processes by which such words had become generally accepted. The publication in Sydney in 1916 of the *Australian Comic Dictionary of Words and Phrases,* by 'Turner O. Lingo' (M. E. Fullerton), again suggests a popular interest in the newly discovered Australian vocabulary.

For the first time, also, a consciousness of the uniqueness of Australian English led to writers providing glossaries for their readers. C. J. Dennis's *Songs of a Sentimental Bloke* (1915) and *The Moods of Ginger Mick* (1916) both carry glossaries which are useful for readers of Dennis's verse but which include many American and English slang words as well as coinages of Dennis's own, like *bellers,*

---

[20] See 'Australianisms and Their Origin', pp. 114-16.

'lungs', *gorspel-cove,* and *handies,* which were probably not used outside his verse. In his biography, A. H. Chisholm discusses Dennis's interest in words and mentions a letter to R. H. Croll dated August 1913, in which Dennis revealed that he had long been collecting words for a dictionary of slang which he intended to publish. This collection was presumably developed into the glossary. At a later date Dennis described how his pride in himself as 'arch-protagonist and chief promulgator of an argot hitherto little known in the English-speaking world' began to disintegrate:

> . . . quite well-meaning people wrote to me pointing out the derivation of this cant word and that. One, for example, was almost pure Yiddish; another came from the old rhyming slang of London thieves; another directly from the secret tongue of Romany. Yet another had been brought across by California's 'forty-niners', who came to Australia during the early gold rushes. And so on, until my beautiful glossary was almost decimated through casualties.[21]

This was a lesson which later writers on Australian English could well have heeded. The glossary itself is useful, being a contemporary record of the slang used in Dennis's verse and, if it is open to misinterpretation, it is not as misleading as a number of glossaries of Australian words designed particularly for an audience interested in migrating to Australia. In 1926, in *Timely Tips for New Australians,* 'Jice Doone' (Vance Marshall) produced the first of these, commenting briefly on the characteristics of the Australian vocabulary and appending a glossary, mainly of slang words, for the use of intending migrants. Marshall is careful to exclude non-Australian words, and

[21] A. H. Chisholm, *Making of a Sentimental Bloke,* quoting from a Melbourne *Herald* of 1934. Chisholm also mentions (p. 80) a short glossary with a note on Australian slang by C. Hartley Grattan appended to *Larrikin,* the American edition of Louis Stone's *Jonah* (1933). Letters in the *Bulletin* of 7 March 1918 and 2 May 1918 argue that Dennis 'faithfully reported the slang in use at the time from Little Lon. to South'.

his definitions are accurate; but his practice seems to have been to include the more colourful words of both the standard and the slang vocabulary without proper concern for their currency. Other glossaries of this type, published since World War II, have been shorter than Marshall's, frequently inaccurate, and seriously misleading in that they too record only the most popularized of Australianisms, words like *billabong, billy, jackeroo,* and *jumbuck,* without proper regard for their currency.[22] Related to these, and not infrequently of some use in ascertaining the usage of a given word, are a number of glossaries in travel books directed primarily to a non-Australian audience or in books, like Ernestine Hill's *The Great Australian Loneliness,* set in parts of Australia unfamiliar to most readers.[23] Most recently, there are those attached to the *Penguin Book of Australian Verse* and the *Penguin Book of Australian Ballads.*[24]

But these glossaries, while they reflect an awareness of the difference of Australian English from British English, are not the result of any fresh inquiry. Nor, with the exception of a vocabulary of war words, is there anything to suggest that the interest in Australian words which Morris's dictionary had aroused survived beyond World War I.[25]

W. H. Downing's *Digger Dialects,* published in Melbourne in 1919, is the first record of Australian services' slang. The vocabulary gives a vivid picture of the language of Australian soldiers of World War I, though Downing

[22] See J. Douglas, *Opportunity in Australia*; D. Walker, *We went to Australia*; and A. E. Mander, *The Making of the Australians.*

[23] See, e.g., T. Wood, *Cobbers*; A. L. Haskell, *Waltzing Matilda*; and C. J. Finger, *A Dog at his Heel.*

[24] Edited, respectively, by J. Thompson, K. Slessor, R. G. Howarth, and by R. Ward.

[25] Occasionally, of course, there have been short, uninquiring newspaper articles. For instance, a vocabulary of slang words was published in *Truth* (Sydney) on 27 April 1924, p. 6, which occupied a full page and was part of a picture game in which readers were asked to match items illustrated on the page with words from the list. And, again, there was a short unsigned article, 'Australia Needs More Slang', in the *Daily Telegraph* (Sydney), 14 July 1936, p. 6.

has not attempted to exclude non-Australian words. Australian slang words which were in use in Australia before
1914 and which are still current are listed, as well as
English words, a number of French and Arabic borrowings, and nonce words which were probably generally
current amongst servicemen. A smaller glossary of war
slang was included in the 1920 edition of *Aussie*.[26]

Digger Dialects represents a response to a particular set
of circumstances and the growth in the slang vocabulary
which it occasioned. But it was not until the thirties that
any resurgence of interest in Australian English generally
became apparent.

In 1933 'A Sheep Station Glossary', compiled by L. G. D.
Acland, was published in *The Press*.[27] This is a glossary
of sheep-farming terms, shearers' slang, and words for
plants and animals and features of the landscape recorded
in Canterbury, New Zealand. Many of the words are
common to Australian and New Zealand English and,
where possible, Acland has indicated derivations. Most
of the Australian borrowings are acknowledged, Acland
having checked his entries against those in Morris.

For a few words Acland either gives quotations or indicates where a quotation can be found, but for most he
gives no evidence, attempting only to indicate from his
own acquaintance with a word the extent of its currency
in New Zealand English. These observations, usually
dating a word as current in the period between 1890 and
1910, are carefully made and the glossary as a whole seems
reliable. There is no comparable record of the Australian
sheep-farming vocabulary, so that Acland's glossary is a
necessary source of reference.

Also published in 1933 was Eric Partridge's *Slang Today
and Yesterday*, which contains a vocabulary of Australian

[26] M. Johnston, 'Aussie Dictionary', *Aussie*, 18 January 1918, pp.
10-11.

[27] Reprinted, with an introduction by Professor Arnold Wall, as
an appendix to L. G. D. Acland's *Early Canterbury Runs*, pp. 355-
411.

C

slang and a short note on the relationship of Australian slang to English and American. The vocabulary is intended to be representative and to give, in addition to definitions, some indication of the currency of the words listed. Partridge's debt to Morris is considerable: almost all the datings of words in use before 1898 are taken from *Austral English,* and the high proportion of obsolete words in the vocabulary seems to result partly from Partridge's retention of little used slang or colloquial words recorded by Morris.[28]

A number of words well established in general Australian usage are included without comment,[29] and the distinction made between these and a few words described as Standard English[30] suggests that Partridge, like Lentzner, has treated as slang all English words not familiar in England. His heavy dependence on Morris and misleading classification of standard Australian words as slang greatly reduce the book's value.

Partridge has not, in later articles, made any more valuable contribution to the subject. His article on Australian English in *The Sunburnt Country*[31] is brief and unscientific, apparently an expansion of an earlier article in *British and American English Since 1900.*[32] The observations made are general and the illustrations given are not always accurate.[33] His most recent article is in *A Charm of Words* (1960). This is, as Partridge says, substantially

---

[28] See, e.g., *Australian flag, badger box, bangtail muster, bush-scrubber, eagle-hawking.* Partridge has drawn also from Marshall's glossary.

[29] For example, *billy, fossick, lubra, outback, ropeable, rouseabout, willy-willy.*

[30] For example, *billabong, buck* (vb.), *bushranger, jackeroo* (described as 'almost S.E.').

[31] Edited by I. Bevan: 'Their Language', pp. 212-23.

[32] *British and American English Since 1900* (edited by E. Partridge and J. W. Clark): 'Australian English', pp. 85-9. There is a more useful article on Australian English by A. K. Thomson in the same volume (pp. 332-6). Both articles are concerned with the emergence of Australian English in this century.

[33] As words probably of Aboriginal origin Partridge lists *billy, boomer, burrawang* (a derivative of a place-name), *dugong,* and *jumbuck.*

the same article as appeared in *The Sunburnt Country* in 1953. Added to it is a short bibliography of works on Australian English and a list of the books which Partridge considers have 'the most influenced or the best exemplified the growth, nature and potentialities of . . . Australian English'. Almost all of these are fictional, and evidence from many of them on questions of usage is of doubtful validity.

Valuable not so much for itself as for its demonstration of a growing interest in Australian English is an unpublished M.A. thesis submitted at the University of Sydney in 1938: J. H. Britton's An Investigation into the Source Materials of Australian Additions to the English Language. In the thesis Britton examines borrowings from non-English sources, borrowings from English sources (e.g. dialect revivals and 'words which have been borrowed from standard English and given extended meanings in Australia'), and words formed in Australia, either by derivation or composition. Britton does not give evidence of the use of the words he examines, is sometimes inaccurate through lack of evidence, and is frequently too concerned with establishing the existence of Australian English; yet the thesis is one of the first serious attempts to describe the distinctive characteristics of Australian English.

Australian services' slang of World War II was the subject of several short and generally unselective newspaper articles,[34] but it is perhaps most fully recorded by Baker. A. G. Mitchell, in 'Fighting Words',[35] discussed the likelihood of World War I slang being revived, but his 'Glossary of War Words'[36] is not restricted to Australian usage. The stationing of American troops in Australia from 1942 led to a popular American interest in Australia and the Australian way of life. Several short articles on Australian words reflect this interest but make no contribution to

[34] See, e.g., G. H. Johnston, 'This War is Evolving New Army Slang', *Argus*, 15 November 1941; J. Quinn, 'Diggers Add to Dictionary', *Sun* (Sydney), 26 August 1942.

[35] *Salt*, 22 December 1941.

[36] *Southerly*, no. 3, 1942.

our knowledge of the history or use of the words discussed.[37]

S. J. Baker's *The Australian Language*, published in Sydney in 1945, was the first comprehensive account of the Australian vocabulary since Morris's dictionary. Earlier, in 1941, Baker had published *A Popular Dictionary of Australian Slang*, an unselective and uninformative word list which drew on earlier slang dictionaries and inherited many of their errors. Much of the material in the *Popular Dictionary* is used in *The Australian Language*, and a later volume, *The Drum*,[38] in which Baker discusses various aspects of the Australian character, contains a glossary made up of essentially the same words as are recorded in *The Australian Language*. In *Australia Speaks*, published in Sydney in 1953 as a supplement to *The Australian Language*, he reviews the contents of the earlier volume and adds a number of words. Most of these are local slang words and many are recorded by Baker from letters received after the publication of *The Australian Language*. Some attempt is made to deal with the names of flora and

[37] See, e.g., 'Aussies' Own Talk', *New York Times Magazine*, 22 March 1942, p. 38; 'Slang Down Under', *New York Times Magazine*, 7 January 1943, p. 31; W. Hicks, 'Australian Slang', *Life*, 18 April 1942, pp. 15-17. Hicks's article draws its material from Baker's *Australian Language*. There are also a number of short articles on Australian English to be found in books surveying the use of English in the twentieth century, but none of these is of more than incidental interest. G. L. Brook, *English Dialects*, pp. 129-33, is the most useful of these; but see also T. H. Pear, *Personality, Appearance and Speech*, pp. 106-8; M. A. Pei, *The World's Chief Languages* (formerly *Languages for War and Peace*), pp. 72-5 (a short comment with a grossly inaccurate slang vocabulary); G. H. McKnight, in *English Words and Their Background*, indicates some of the differences between Australian and American English, and there are brief notes on the character and affiliations of Australian English in H. L. Mencken, *American Language*, p. 378, and A. C. Baugh, *A History of the English Language*, pp. 394-5. There is a short article by D. O'Meara, 'Australian "Cobber" ', in *American Speech*, vol. 21 (December 1946), no. 4, p. 273; O'Meara suggests a Hebrew derivation for the word *cobber*.

[38] Only current words are supposed to be in this glossary; critically reviewed by A. Delbridge, *Southerly*, no. 1, 1961, pp. 50-1.

fauna[39] and with the possible effects of immigrants on Australian English, subjects not fully considered in the earlier volume. In several short articles on specific topics Baker has again drawn on material used in *The Australian Language*.[40]

Baker defines as an Australianism every expression that has originated in Australia and every new meaning given to expressions used in England or in other parts of the world; his intention, in *The Australian Language*,[41] was to describe the occurrence of these expressions in the popular speech of Australians. All except the most com-

[39] There is in the Mitchell Library, Sydney, a typescript copy of a Dictionary of Australian Flora and Fauna, by S. J. Baker, dated 1950. This is a word list, mainly of popular names, without adequate definitions and with no illustrative material.

[40] See the articles in the *Encyclopaedia Britannica* (1950 ed.) and in the *Australian Encyclopaedia*, ed. A. H. Chisholm, on Australian Slang and Pidgin English; 'The Influence of American Slang on Australian', *American Speech*, vol. 18 (December 1943), pp. 253-6; 'The Literature of Pidgin English', *American Speech*, vol. 19 (December 1944), no. 4; 'Australian Rhyming Argot in the American Underworld', *American Speech*, vol. 19 (October 1944), pp. 183-95; 'Home-Grown Idiom Goes to Work', *Sydney Morning Herald*, 18 October 1952; 'Language and Character', in *Australian Signpost, an Anthology* (ed. T. A. G. Hungerford), pp. 175-9 (also reprinted in *The Drum*, pp. 41-7); 'Language', in A. L. McLeod, *The Pattern of Australian Culture*, pp. 102-30.

[41] Reviewed by R. M. Wilson in the *Year's Work in English Studies*, vol. 27 (1946), pp. 56-7; R. J. Menner in *American Speech*, vol. 21 (April 1946), pp. 120-2; and R. E. Spiller in *Saturday Review of Literature*, vol. 29, (19 January 1946), no. 3, p. 12. These reviewers are faced with the same difficulty as Swaen, in his review of Lentzner's dictionary: with no suitable source of reference to use in comparison and no first-hand knowledge of the subject they are unable to assess properly Baker's principles of inclusion and exclusion. Wilson remarks on Baker's failure to distinguish slang words from standard. In an excellent critical review, 'Lingo-Jingo', *Southerly*, no. 2 (1946), pp. 97-103, J. Ackroyd notices Baker's use of insufficient evidence, his 'patriotism', his inclusion of obsolescent or locally used words, and his turgid style. Cf. also A. Clunies Ross's review in *Australian Quarterly*, December 1945, pp. 123-5, which is critical of Baker's 'missionary' attitude towards his subject and of his indiscriminate collecting of slang.

mon of the names of flora and fauna were thus placed
outside the scope of inquiry.

Discussion of the vocabulary is divided into chapters on
words grouped according to their area of usage, subject
matter, or source of origin.[42] Parts 3 and 4 describe,
respectively, the use of idiom in Australian literature and
the characteristics of Australian pronunciation.[43] Baker
has been an enthusiastic collector and the vocabulary recorded in *The Australian Language* is more extensive than
that of any earlier study. For this reason alone the book is
useful. Baker has recorded instances of many words used
earlier than Morris's quotations suggest, and this dating,
together with Baker's grouping of the words, gives an
indication of the period and the type of source material
in which further evidence of a word's use is likely to be
found.

But his enthusiasm as a collector has led to many inaccuracies. In the manner of some early American lexicographers he has striven to show the vigour and independence of the language he is describing and to indicate from
this something of the character of the people who use it.
The large and varied vocabulary he has recorded includes
words which are not Australian[44] and words which, though
probably Australian, have never had more than a limited

[42] For example, there are chapters on the vocabularies of sheep
and cattle farming, bush idiom and war slang; on names of flora
and fauna, 'pastimes and pleasures'; and on Aboriginal words, and
those of overseas origin.

[43] Part 4 (pp. 319-58), which describes Australian pronunciation,
is unscientific and inaccurate; cf. also his *Australian Pronunciation*.

[44] For example *alec, bach, brush, bushranger, to dice* 'throw
away', *to drop* 'the act of giving birth', *to face* 'in arranging goods
for sale', *to job, lurk,* and many others. Significant also is the
rigidity with which Baker accepts the principle that 'textual quotations are sufficient evidence upon which to base the original
currency of a word' (p. 277): *brush* and *bush* and *bushranger* are
classed as Australian on the evidence of Australian quotations earlier
than those given in Craigie and Hulbert's *Dictionary of American
English*. Mathews's *Dictionary of Americanisms* contains fresh
evidence on the American use of these words and it is clearly unwise
to be too dogmatic about the origin of words found in use in
Australia and America at the same time.

currency.[45] It is important to have some record of these words but misleading to describe them as Australian.

The amount of information given about the meaning, currency and origin of words varies greatly. Words like *cocky, crawler, squatter,* and *wowser,* which have an interesting or amusing history, are discussed in detail. Many others are simply listed as synonyms or derivatives of a 'key-word',[46] and a number of words, some commonly used here but probably not known outside Australia, are listed with no explanation.[47] Frequently the date of the first recorded use is given with no indication of where the quotation can be found. With a few exceptions slang words are not distinguished from standard: though Lake and Morris both made the distinction without apparent difficulty, Baker argues that it is not yet possible to 'make a cut-and-dried differentiation between standard words and those that fall into the more popular section of our language'.[48]

There are serious weaknesses in Baker's approach and in his method but, although the need for more scholarly descriptions of Australian English is plain, his work should not be disregarded. He has scanned a wide range of primary sources, many of his notes are illuminating and

[45] Baker (*The Australian Language,* p. 126) lists, with dates 'when they came into printed use' the following derivatives of *bonzer: bons* (1904); *bonster* (1904); *bonsterina* (1904); *bontoger* (1904); *bontogerino* (1908); *bontosher* (1904); and *bonzerina* (1906). There is nothing to distinguish the currency of these forms, probably used once or twice in the *Bulletin,* from that of the well established *bonzer.*

[46] Derivatives of *station* are listed (op. cit., p. 60) without further comment: *heifer station* (1845), *head station* (1848), *home station* (1853), *outstation* (1846), *outside station* (1878), and *backstation* (1890). Synonyms of *to borrow* are listed without further comment (p. 107): *to put the acid on, to put the hard word on, to sting, nibble or nip a person, to put the drags on.*

[47] For example, the Aboriginal words *kookaburra, leangle, lubra, mulga, waratah, warrigal, wilga, wonga wonga.* Also *pigrooting, Pacific slope* ('standard'), *Hawkesbury duck, hutkeeper, anabranch* (not in fact Australian), *bull-roarer.*

[48] *The Australian Language,* p. 242.

his vocabulary, once its excesses are recognized, makes a useful complement to Morris's dictionary.

Since 1945 a handful of short and uninformed articles, testimony to continued popular interest, have appeared in American and English journals on 'curiosities' of Australian English.[49] But the most important development has been the formation at Sydney University of the Australian Language Research Centre. Interest in Australian English had, from the thirties, continued to develop at Sydney. E. R. Holme revised the Australian entries for the 1935 edition of *Webster's*,[50] and in 1946 the first edition of A. G. Mitchell's book, *The Pronunciation of English in Australia* (revised in 1965 by A. Delbridge) was published. Mitchell's interest was in recording the characteristics of Australian pronunciation and in seeking out evidence of its historical development, rather than in lexicography, but his *Supplement of Australian and New Zealand Words*, published in the Australian edition of *Chambers's Shorter English Dictionary*, is important. The dictionary is popular, intended as 'a general reference work for the ordinary, non-specialist reader', and for this reason the *Supplement* is not intended to be exhaustive. Very little historical detail is included. Yet the *Supplement*'s definitions are reliable and it is the first vocabulary since Lake's

[49] T. Harrison, for example, in the *New Statesman and Nation* (23 November 1946, p. 375) has a note on *wowser* and its compounds *grog wowser*, *sheila wowser*, *Sunday wowser* and *Cinewowser*; he remarks that 'most digger slang is immediately comprehensible to the Pommy, as an abbreviated enrichment of crypto-cockney'. An unsigned article in the *Rotarian* (June 1946, p. 36) 'Cooee this is fair dinkum', and an article by C. R. Bradish in the *American Mercury* (July 1954, pp. 72-4), 'The Australian Vernacular', comment on the strangeness and vividness of Australian slang. Both writers illustrate their comments by translating American idiom into Australian, quite inaccurately. A more serious and far more important article on the make-up of the Australian vocabulary is J. Sharwood and S. Gerson, 'The Vocabulary of Australian English', *Moderna Språk*, vol. LVII, pp. 1-10. One should note also F. J. Schonell, I. G. Meddleton, and B. A. Shaw, *A Study of the Oral Vocabulary of Adults*, a frequency list based on the usage of Australian workers.

[50] See A. G. Mitchell, *Sydney Morning Herald*, 20 April 1935, p. 7.

which gives a balanced and properly selected record of Australian English.[51] As a professor of English at the University of Sydney until 1962, Mitchell has stimulated scholarly interest and research into both the pronunciation and the vocabulary of Australian English and the formation of the Australian Language Research Centre, where for the first time a full-scale investigation of the sounds and vocabulary of Australian English has been begun, must be seen as an outcome of his continued interest and activity.[52] But it will, of course, be some time before the

[51] See also an article on the emergence of Australian English, 'Australian English', *Australian Quarterly*, vol. xxiii (March 1951), pp. 9-17 (and subsequent correspondence in *Australian Quarterly*, June 1951, pp. 115-16, and March 1952, pp. 77-81). Mitchell's *Australian Accent*, an address to the Australian Humanities Research Council in November 1960 mainly reports on more recent investigations into Australian pronunciation but has some interesting comments on the growth of the vocabulary. Other dictionaries for use in Australia have followed *Chambers's*; see, for instance, Whitcombe and Tombs's *A Modern Junior Dictionary* and Collins's *New Gem Dictionary*.

[52] The Centre's first venture has been the publication of a series of occasional papers reporting on work in progress. Already published are: G. H. Russell, *The University of Sydney Australian Language Research Centre: An Introduction*; R. D. Eagleson, *Australianisms in Early Migrant Handbooks, 1788-1826*; W. S. Ramson, *The Currency of Aboriginal Words in Australian English*; R. D. Eagleson, *Australianisms in Early Migrant Handbooks, 1827-1830*; J. S. Gunn, *The Terminology of the Shearing Industry*; and J. R. Bernard, *The Rate of Utterance in Australian Dialect Groups*.

Other publications by members of the Centre include: J. R. Bernard, 'The Need for a Dictionary of Australian English', *Southerly*, no. 2 (1962); R. D. Eagleson, 'Contemporary Evidence of the Connexion Between Word and Meaning', *Notes and Queries* (N.S.), vol. ii, no. 2, pp. 70-1; 'Naming a Currency. A Study of Contemporary Methods of Word Creation', *Southerly*, no. 4 (1963), pp. 264-70; A. Delbridge, 'The Use of English in Australian Literature', *Harvard Educational Review*, vol. 34(2), (1964), pp. 306-11; W. S. Ramson, 'Aboriginal Words in Early Australian English', *Southerly*, no. 1 (1964), pp. 50-60; 'Australian Aboriginal Words in the O.E.D.', *Notes and Queries* (N.S.), vol. ii, no. 2, pp. 69-70; *Australian English*, Commonwealth Literary Fund Lecture 1964; 'A Critical Review of Writings on the Vocabulary of Australian Eng-

material necessary for a full and accurate record of the vocabulary can be assembled.

3

Primary Sources

An historical study of the Australian English vocabulary must be based on a wide range of sources. These would, in a study of contemporary usage, include spoken as well as written sources, transcripts and recordings of Australian speech being particularly important in determining the present currency of colloquial words and occupational terms. But documents which purport to be transcripts of nineteenth-century Australian speech have usually been subject to editing; no great reliance can be placed on their accuracy and the lexicographer must establish the history of a word's use almost entirely from written sources.

Sources for the period up until 1830 are fewer and of a narrower range than the sources for later periods: there is almost no fictional writing and the spate of books describing the colony and giving advice to emigrants had barely begun. Among the most useful sources for the early period are the Governors' despatches to the Colonial Office, the letters and journals of missionaries sent to the missionary societies in London, the journals of members of the First Fleet, men like Tench, Collins, Southwell, and White, and of other early settlers and visitors like Cunningham, whose *Two Years in New South Wales* (1827), contains useful information on social conditions in the colony.

Despatches from the Governors of the colonies are full of information on a wide range of topics.[1] They are often lengthy, with paragraphs describing the appearance and growth of the colony, recent events and transactions. There are frequently enclosures, documents and letters pertain-

[1] See *Historical Records of Australia (H.R.A.)*, Series I. All references to *H.R.A.* are to 'Series I', which is henceforth omitted.

ing to the subject matter of the despatch. The most useful despatches are those which report on the Aborigines, on exploration and travel, on land transactions, and on the establishment and progress of settlements in outlying districts. The language is formal, so that the occurrence of words like *run, station, stockman* and *stockyard* without comment seems a fair indication that these words were in general use in the colony. Colloquial words like *croppy*, for 'convict', and *waddy*, 'a club', are not common but are sometimes found in the more informal enclosures, such as letters from settlers and accounts of court proceedings.

As the population increased and the administration of the colony became more complex the character of the despatches changed and their usefulness for vocabulary study declines: the Governor's dealings with settlers lost the intimacy which belongs to a small community and the despatches became more and more concerned with administrative matters. The despatches of the Governors of New South Wales hold little interest for the lexicographer after the 1830s.

Non-fictional descriptions of Australia in explorers' journals, and in the journals and letters of settlers, travellers, and missionaries often contain valuable lexicographical information. The usefulness of these sources depends on the writer's powers of observation, on his familiarity with the people or part of Australia of which he is writing, and on the formality of the style he adopts. Thus the range of Australian words used by G. C. Mundy in *Our Antipodes* (1852), is much smaller than that used by W. Howitt in *Land, Labour and Gold, or Two Years in Victoria* (1855), though both writers base their accounts closely on the journals they kept in Australia. Mundy's style is discursive and literary and his descriptions lack the precision of Howitt's. He does not observe people as closely as Howitt, who reports in detail their behaviour, dress and language.

One of the most useful of the explorers' journals is T. L. Mitchell's *Three Expeditions into the Interior of Eastern Australia* (1838); and the comparison between this and A. Cunningham's Tour into the Interior of New South Wales is instructive.[2] Cunningham first traversed parts of northern New South Wales but he does not seem to have observed the flora and fauna closely or to have made contact with the Aborigines. His journal is of no importance lexicographically. Mitchell, on the other hand, was a trained observer who made notes on the flora, fauna, and geology of the regions he traversed and who made a point of ascertaining the local Aboriginal names for the rivers, hills, and other features of the landscape, and for the flora and fauna of the region. He first records *goborro*, in a vocabulary of the language used in the Wellington Valley, and *quondong* and *yarra* in a vocabulary of the language used in the Lachlan district, and later uses these words, along with the botanical names, in his journal. Mitchell also notes *Billibang*, the Aboriginal name of the Bell River, from which *billabong* is almost certainly derived. Explorers' journals are unlikely to provide lexicographical information about words other than the names of flora and fauna and place-names, but it is useful not only to be able to trace these but also to have some record of a process of borrowing from Aboriginal languages which is the result of a deliberate attempt to retain the Aboriginal name.

The journals and letters of settlers also seem a likely source of information, particularly on words from the vocabularies of sheep and cattle stations. These again vary greatly in their usefulness, as one collection, T. F. Bride's *Letters from Victorian Pioneers* (1898) indicates. The letters were written in answer to a circular letter from Lieutenant-Governor La Trobe, requesting information on the settlement of parts of Victoria. Some writers give the barest details of their arrival in the colony and occupation of a run; others give quite lengthy descriptions of their experiences. Some use Australian words freely: C. B. Hall, for instance, in a letter written in 1853, uses a number of Australian words which must have been in general currency, a few colloquialisms and one or two short passages of Aboriginal pidgin, so that his letter is of

[2] 1827; MS., Sturt Collection, Rhodes House, Oxford.

real interest lexicographically.[3] It is probable that letters from settlers in Australia to their families or close friends in Britain would contain more words of a colloquial nature than these relatively formal letters to the Victorian Governor; such letters or collections of letters, if they become accessible, should be a valuable source.

The journals of English visitors to Australia before 1850 may also be useful. One of the earliest of these, D. Collins's *Account of the English Colony in New South Wales* (1798), for example, contains descriptions of the first contacts made with the Aborigines: Collins records one of the earliest vocabularies of an Aboriginal language and, in the text of his journal, uses Aboriginal names for flora and fauna and for weapons, dwellings, and other features of Aboriginal life. His notes, intended to explain these words to an English public to whom they are not familiar, are often useful. Letters and journals of missionaries, for example J. Gunther's Journal, 1836-40,[4] can also be important in establishing borrowings from Aboriginal languages. But few of the journals written before about 1850 contain slang or colloquial words. J. Backhouse's *Narrative of a Visit to the Australian Colonies* (1843), for instance, is written in formal, almost literary English; the writer accepts Aboriginal words and non-colloquial words like *bush, run, station, stockman* and *stock station*, which were in general use in New South Wales, but does not as a rule use or record the slang or colloquial speech of convicts and immigrants. Only occasionally does one of the visitors give us a tantalizing glimpse of the language of 'the other half': Alexander Marjoribanks, in 1847, pauses to reflect on the Australian use of *bloody*. It is, he says,

the favourite oath in that country. One may tell you

---

[3] For example, *to boil down, cattle run, cormorant squattocracy, corroboree, crawler* (of cattle), *hutkeeper, kangaroo-tail soup, lubra, mia mia, run, sheep station, station, stockyard,* and *waterhole*; also the sentence, 'I believe blackfellow bimbulalee sheep all about, then whitefellow gilbert and put 'em along o' fire'.

[4] MS., Mitchell Library.

that he married a bloody young wife, another, a bloody old one; and a bushranger will call out, 'Stop, or I'll blow your bloody brains out.'

Marjoribanks records having heard a bullock-driver use *bloody* twenty-five times in a quarter of an hour and calculates that, at this rate, allowing eight hours a day for sleep and six for silence, and assuming that he became a fully-fledged swearer at 20 and died at 70, he would in the course of those fifty years 'have pronounced this disgusting word no less than 18,200,000 times'.[5] But this was the full extent of Marjoribanks's investigations into Australian colloquial speech.

Journals of the goldrush period and later differ in this respect. Colloquial words had had more time to establish themselves in general usage and, what was probably more important, the social upheaval of the period had meant that upper-class English travellers met on the roads and diggings men of all classes with whom they had previously had little contact in Australia. Early descriptions of the goldfields are the most important sources of evidence for the use of the large number of gold-digging terms in Australian English. But popular accounts, like C. R. Read's *What I Heard, Saw, and Did at the Australian Gold Fields* (1853), are important for their record of the slang and colloquial speech heard on the diggings as well as for their record of gold-digging terms.

Other interesting non-fictional sources of information on the use of Australian words are the handbooks of advice to emigrants. These contain information on a wide range of topics and seem generally to have been written by Englishmen who had visited Australia. In *Hetherington's Useful Handbook for Intending Emigrants* (n.d.), there are many Australian words but some of these are obviously used to create an impression of authenticity; sources of this sort do not always provide reliable evidence of the currency of Australian words.

There are many handbooks from the 1840s on and it

[5] *Travels in New South Wales*, pp. 57-8.

is clear that other books not specifically addressed to emigrants are intended for the same public. Alexander Harris's
Settlers and Convicts (1847) is one of these. Harris's narrative describes his experiences as a cedar-sawyer, his
search for and establishment of a cattle station, and his
many adventures with bushrangers, convicts, criminals in
Sydney, cattle-thieves, and wild Aborigines. In the course
of this narrative he uses an extensive vocabulary of slang
and colloquial words.

At several points the narrative is broken to enable
Harris to give advice to intending emigrants. Thus he
describes a new settler's failure to run a cattle station and
goes on to 'contrast with the dismal tale a statement of the
course which a new settler should pursue'.[6] His statement
is one of detailed advice on the selection of land, the
engaging of men, the purchase of stock, the erection of
buildings and clearing of land, and the treatment of the
Aborigines. Australian words used in this passage include
bale (milking), *bough yard, bush cow, dray, hutkeeper,
native dog, overseer* (of a station), *paddock, run, stockyard*
and *waterhole*.

The journals of explorers, new settlers, travellers, and
missionaries are frequently useful because the writers
record words which are to them new or unfamiliar, sometimes words which may have had a limited currency.
Aboriginal words recorded by explorers or missionaries,
for instance, may have been used in one part of Australia
only. The words recorded by explorers are likely to be
names of useful or striking flora and fauna; by missionaries,
names of flora and fauna and of Aboriginal customs, dwellings, and implements. Words recorded by new settlers are
likely to be the names of flora and fauna or words used in
a particular occupation.

Handbooks of information for intending emigrants and
gold-diggers, on the other hand, may be useful because
writers have drawn extensively on the vocabulary of
Australian English, describing a wide range of occupations

[6] *Settlers and Convicts* (ed. C. M. H. Clark), p. 155.

in their own terms and using slang or colloquial words where these seemed appropriate. Yet evidence from source material of this sort cannot be accepted without question; in the latter part of the century, especially, writers often deliberately used Australianisms for their stylistic effect.

Early newspapers, like the Governors' despatches, provide a continuous record of a wide range of happenings in the colony, and evidence from these sources can usefully supplement that from journals, letters, and handbooks for emigrants. In each of the colonies the publication of a newspaper followed closely on the establishment of a settlement, Sydney's first being published in 1803, Hobart's in 1810, Perth's in 1831, Adelaide's in 1837, Melbourne's in 1838, and Brisbane's in 1846. A good part of the *Sydney Gazette*, which may be regarded as typical of other early newspapers in its layout and content, was occupied by General Orders, extracts from newspapers arriving in the colony and shipping news. Of local interest were reports of events in the colony, trial reports, and advertisements, and it is clearly only in these that Australian words will be found. There is a short note in the *Sydney Gazette* of 9 October 1803, for instance, on the new quadruped, the *koolah*, while an advertisement in the issue for 12 February 1804 offers for sale 'a commodious dwelling-house' with 'an extensive *run* for stock'.[7] But generally the style of writing is formal and the diction conservative, and it seems unlikely that new or colloquial words would occur with great frequency. Many of the advertisements concern lost stock, or stock, properties, and buildings for sale and it is probable that the early use of words like *run* could be documented from this source. The first country newspapers to be published were the *Tasmanian* (1825) and the *Hunter River Gazette* (1841). Evidence from other sources suggests that a good part of the vocabulary of sheep-farming was in use before 1850, so it is probable that a reading of the relevant sections of country newspapers

---

[7] *Koolah* (*koala*) is recorded elsewhere in 1802 and 1803. The next recorded occurrence of *run* is in a Governor's despatch of 1822.

D

and of the *Sydney Gazette* would provide useful information about this.

From 1850 onwards a great volume of source material is available which is more accessible and of greater potential use than newspapers. Popular accounts of life on the goldfields are likely to employ a greater number of colloquial words, and possibly of technical words, than newspaper accounts of gold discoveries and rushes. Accounts of station life and activities in handbooks for intending emigrants and in letters and journals of settlers probably use more of the occupational terms and names of flora and fauna than are to be found in reports of local news in newspapers. Yet there are times when a reading of newspapers is useful. There is little doubt, for instance, that an examination of the earliest paper reports of the goldrushes, particularly those published in the new goldmining towns, would provide additional evidence of the currency of goldmining terms.

In general, the language used in periodicals published before 1880 has characteristics similar to those of the novels and poetry of the period. The diction is literary and 'elevated', the expression formal. Australian words are rare. Even after 1850, when many occupational terms and Aboriginal borrowings had become established and writers like Alexander Harris had used them effectively in fictional and non-fictional writings, the character of the periodicals does not seem to change. Many re-publish articles and stories from English periodicals, and those articles and stories which are locally written are commonly on subjects not specifically Australian. The few Australian words that are used, words like *bush, creek, paddock, stockman,* and *woolshed,* extensions of the meanings of older English words and simple compounds, were generally current but seem to have been used deliberately as Australianisms. Evidence of this restraint can be seen in an excerpt from the *Colonial Literary Journal* of July 1844, in which an anonymous correspondent offers two translations of a German poem, the first into a stereotyped poetic diction, the second into 'Australian English'. *Cottage* is replaced by *bark hut, verdant lea* by *a patch of maize, brook* by *creek, tree* by *wattle, nightingale* by *cocky-bird* and *rising wind* by *brickfielder.* The editor adds: 'We insert this at the request of an anonymous Correspondent, as we think the Colonial manner in which he has translated the Ode will amuse our country subscribers.'[8]

The *Bulletin* of the nineties comes as something of a contrast, with writers like Lawson, 'Steele Rudd' and the anonymous writers of ballads, songs and anecdotes using Australianisms without restraint. As Vance Palmer wrote, the *Bulletin*'s editor during the nineties, J. F. Archibald, drew

> into his pages all who had something to say about their
> work or the life in which they were immersed—the
> shearer, the swagman, the government official, the en-
> gineer; he allowed them to talk in their own idiom,
> pointed their paragraphs, made them feel that the paper
> was their forum.[9]

There was a lively interest in words and, especially after the publication of Morris's *Austral English*, a number of letters and notes appeared in which the use and etymology of outback words were discussed.

Yet the usefulness of much of this is questionable. Many of the slang and colloquial words used had only a local and short-lived currency. A few, like *aboriginality* and *binghi*, were used only in the *Bulletin* or by writers who have been contributors to the *Bulletin*.[10] There was a tendency to pack short, anecdotal passages, especially those published in the 'Aboriginalities' column, with slang and colloquial words. A form of 'elegant variation' was common, a num-ber of synonyms being used in a short passage for the

---

[8] *Colonial Literary Journal*, vol. 1 (July 1844), p. 62.

[9] Vance Palmer, *The Legend of the Nineties*, p. 91.

[10] Baker culled the following expressions for the *outback* from copies of the *Bulletin*: *back-of-beyond, wayback, rightback, back-o' Bourke, back-o' outback, beyond outback, behind out-back, set-o' sun, death-o' day, past-west, westest-west, beyond set-o' sun, right behind death-o' day, right at the rear of back-of-outback* (*The Australian Language*, p. 57). Only a few of these have been in general use.

object or person described.[11] The *Bulletin* anecdotes in this way acquired a strong outback flavour but they were not accurate representations of outback speech, still less of Australian speech generally.

As a general rule evidence from literary sources is not as useful as that from non-fictional sources. Most writers before about 1880 used the vocabulary of nineteenth-century literary English, introducing Australian words only occasionally and then more for local colour than for any other reason. In Charles Rowcroft's *The Bushranger of Van Diemen's Land* (1843), for example, no attempt is made to represent the speech of the colony and only a few Australian words are used in passages of natural description. The naturalness with which these occur can be judged from one passage in which an Englishman, newly arrived in Tasmania, descends into a 'gulley', recoils in horror from a 'Tasmanian devil', stumbles over a 'wombat' as he makes his escape and emerges from a thicket to meet, and enterprisingly engage in combat, a 'boomah'.[12]

An unknown writer in the *Journal of Australasia* remarked in 1856 that, although most people had had more than enough of 'positive Australian dialogue', it had not yet been 'artistically reported';[13] and the distance between reality and literary representation is well indicated by a passage from Kingsley's *Recollections of Geoffrey Hamlyn* (p. 181) in which the best abuse one of the convicts can muster up is:

[11] For example, 'Bushmen have some ingenious ways of curing a *horse* of the habit of bridle-breaking. Some hobble the *moke*, then pass the reins over a rail and buckle them to the hobble rings. After *Carbine* has pulled his front feet from under himself and toppled over a couple of times, he thinks the reins are on his feet if they are only dropped on the ground, and will stand anywhere. A man who owned a chronic *bridlesmasher* put a post in on the sloping bank of a dam, and tied the *brumby* to the lower side of it with a rope that would stand a good strain. When it broke, the astonished *prad* plunged suddenly into the dam. Two doses of that remedy and he was a reformed *animal.*' *Bulletin*, 27 December 1933, p. 20 (my italics).

[12] Vol. 1, pp. 130-2.

[13] Quoted in Baker, *The Australian Language*, p. 302.

'Oh, my ———— colonial oath! Oh my ———— cabbage tree! So there's going to be a coil about that scrubby little myrnonger, eh? Don't you fret your bingy, boss; he'll be as good a man as his father yet!'

The awful falseness of this passage must have struck even Kingsley, for he adds a footnote saying that, as a specimen of colonial slang, this is not in the least exaggerated.

For similar reasons much early Australian poetry is unlikely to provide evidence of the use or currency of Australian words. Harpur and Kendall, it is true, switched from traditional themes to the description and interpretation of Australian scenery, yet both retained the conventional vocabulary of English nature poetry. Words like *dell, glade, glen,* and *brook,* seldom found in the prose of the period, are used to describe features of the Australian landscape, and the use of a small number of Australianisms often seems deliberate and awkward.

Yet even before 1850 there were writers who were using the everyday idiom of the Australian bushman without any apparent self-consciousness. Alexander Harris's *The Emigrant Family, or The Story of an Australian Settler* (1849), is a good example. Harris makes his Australian setting an important part of the novel, not simply a background, uninhabited except by wild Aborigines, for the telling of extravagant and melodramatic adventures. The vocabulary of *The Emigrant Family* and that of *Settlers and Convicts,* Harris's earlier book, make an interesting comparison. There are passages of Aboriginal pidgin in *The Emigrant Family* but otherwise no more colloquial words; there are more words from the vocabularies of timber-getting, farming, and grazing in *Settlers and Convicts,* most of these occurring in passages describing and giving advice on these activities. But many words from the vocabularies are the same and Harris's use in the two books of what is substantially the same vocabulary of Australian words suggests that the representation of Australian speech in the dialogue is fairly reliable.

Against the background of other fictional sources, then,

Harris's record of the Australian vocabulary becomes important, not simply for its accuracy but for its range and extensiveness, and also for the fact that here, for the first time, there is a synthesis of the different levels of the vocabulary. Earlier writers have tended to use one level, barely hinting at the existence of another, or crossing occasionally and uneasily between the two, but Harris, whether he is rhapsodizing over an early morning on the Hawkesbury or reporting a bit of skulduggery in Aboriginal pidgin, has adopted the new vocabulary and writes in it with ease and certainty. He is indeed, in the most literal sense of the expression, 'the firste fyndere of oure faire longage'.

Evidence from Harris, supported by that from non-fictional sources, suggests that the impression given by most literary sources before 1880 is false and that there was already in use quite an extensive vocabulary of slang and colloquialisms, popular names for flora and fauna, and occupational terms of the outback. The vocabulary of *Robbery Under Arms* corroborates this. Like Harris, Boldrewood wrote unaffectedly, and the extensive use of colloquialisms and dialect borrowings does not seem to have been made with stylistic effects in mind.

There are, then, a number of literary sources, novels particularly, which may provide evidence on matters of currency and usage. But as a general rule those written before the 1880s tend to be less useful than non-fictional sources because they retain a conventional literary vocabulary, while those written later tend to be less reliable because of the unreal currency given by the *Bulletin* school of writers to a stereotyped 'Australian' vocabulary.

Just as the occurrence of a word in conversation is no proof of its general currency, so the occurrence of a word in a written source is not something which can always be accepted uncritically.

4

The Language of the Settlers: Survivals

ALMOST ALL of the settlers who came before the gold-rushes began in the fifties were from the British Isles; so, before we can decide what is new and distinctive in early Australian English, we must look at the vocabulary they brought with them and determine its relation to the complex of regional and social dialects which at the end of the eighteenth century made up British English. The differences between Australian English and British English result both from the innovations and adaptations the settlers made and from the peculiar composition of the vocabulary with which they left England.

Most of the journals of early administrators and visitors were written in a disciplined prose, whose affinities were with the literary prose of the time, and not with the casual, conversational prose we might expect in a daily journal. It helps to establish the climate in which these early Australian journals were written if we remember that in the year the New South Wales settlement was founded the last volume of Gibbon's *Decline and Fall* was published. Boswell's *Life of Samuel Johnson* appeared in 1791, two years earlier than Tench's *Complete Account of the Settlement at Port Jackson*. Burke's *Reflections on the Revolution in France* was published in 1790, Lamb's *Essays of Elia* in 1823, Cobbett's *Rural Rides* in 1830. The vogue for 'terror' novels continued, Mrs Radcliffe's *Mysteries of Udolpho* being published in 1794, Lewis's *The Monk* in 1795. *Pride and Prejudice* appeared in 1813, *Waverley* in 1814.

These prose works indicate something of the cultivated usage of the time. Of more direct relevance is Johnson's

Dictionary of the English Language (first published in 1755), the eighth edition of which appeared the year before the settlers embarked. Johnson's dictionary was not, like any good dictionary published now, an unbiased record of the vocabulary in use in a given area. Conceived at a time when proposals to found an English academy on the model of the French were still being made, the dictionary was at first intended to establish rather than to record usage, to purify the vocabulary from all slang and colloquial 'barbarisms', and to regularize the meanings of words, their spellings and grammatical functions; in short, to refine the language and to 'fix' it, putting 'a stop to those alterations which time and chance have hitherto been suffered to make in it without opposition'.

Johnson himself came to realize the futility of these aims, but the attitudes which led to his compilation of the dictionary persisted for a long time, the refined usage of a well-bred and well-educated person, the sort of English heard at the Court and in fashionable circles, being kept jealously apart from provincial usage and from common, vulgar usage. As Thomas Sheridan wrote in 1763:

Not only the Scotch, Irish and Welsh have each their own idioms, which uniformly prevail in those countries, but almost every county in England, has its peculiar dialect. Nay in the very metropolis two different modes of pronunciation prevail, by which the inhabitants of one part of the town, are distinguished from those of the other. One is current in the city, and is called the cockney; the other at the court-end, and is called the polite pronunciation. As amongst these various dialects, one must have the preference, and become fashionable, it will of course fall to the lot of that which prevails at court, the source of fashions of all kinds. All other dialects, are sure marks, either of a provincial, rustic, pedantic, or mechanic education; and therefore have some degree of disgrace annexed to them. And as the court pronunciation is no where methodically taught, and can be acquired only by conversing with people in polite life, it is a sort of proof that a person has kept good company, and on that account is sought after by all, who wish to be considered as fashionable people, or members of the beau monde.[1]

That the writers of early New South Wales journals thought of themselves as belonging to this 'polite life' is made clear by their frequent derogatory comments on the English heard in the colony and by their reluctance to use any word which had the slightest taint of slang about it. Tench commented on the 'flash or kiddy language' of the convicts (see p. 108 below), Cunningham on the Billingsgate slang which the Aborigines excelled in using (see p. 108 below). As Edward Gibbon Wakefield wrote, admittedly without first-hand knowledge:

> Bearing in mind that our lowest class brought with it a peculiar language, and is constantly supplied with fresh corruption, you will understand why pure English is not, and is not likely to become, the language of the colony.[2]

We must remember, then, that almost without exception the early journals and accounts of the colony were written in the refined English of educated, upper-class people, that their attitude to the slang and colloquial speech of the lower classes remained as it had been in England, and that large areas of usage—the speech of the convicts and of many of the assisted immigrants—consequently remain uncharted.

The eighth edition of Johnson's dictionary was published in 1786. In the following year Francis Grose, 'the greatest antiquary, joker, and porter-drinker of his day', as one critic described him,[3] and father of the Francis Grose who became Lieutenant-Governor of New South Wales in 1792, published his *Provincial Glossary* and, in 1788, the second edition of his *Classical Dictionary of the Vulgar Tongue*. Grose's attitudes to regional dialect speech

[1] T. Sheridan, *A Course of Lectures on Elocution*, Lecture II (as quoted in S. Tucker, *English Examined*, p. 106).

[2] *A Letter from Sydney*, p. 51.

[3] J. C. Hotten, as quoted in F. Grose, *The Classical Dictionary of the Vulgar Tongue* (ed. E. Partridge), p. 385.

and to the slang of the city were those of his class. He talks
of provincial words

> only retained in counties remote from the capital, where
> modern refinements do not easily find their way, and
> are not readily adopted [and of words] so corrupted by
> passing through the mouths of illiterate clowns as to
> render their origin scarcely discoverable.[4]

The stress is on the utility of such glossaries of the unre-
fined and barbarous:

> The many vulgar allusions and cant expressions that so
> frequently occur in our common conversation and peri-
> odical publications, make a work of this kind extremely
> useful, if not absolutely necessary, not only to foreigners
> but even to natives resident at a distance from the
> Metropolis, or who do not mix in the busy world.[5]

Grose's dictionaries are a sign of the growing interest in
non-standard forms of English and, however incomplete
and undiscriminating they may be, serve to remind us of
the character and status of widely used but largely unrecorded provincial dialect and slang vocabularies.

The linguistic situation, then, is complex. There were
a large number of regional dialects in use in the British
Isles. In any given dialect area there would have been a
range of speakers, from those whose usage was close in all
respects to the 'polite' norm of cultivated speech, to those
'broad' dialect speakers who, in pronunciation, usage, and
vocabulary, were distinctively local and relatively unin-
fluenced by external standards. Nor were the boundaries
between these dialect areas clearly defined: some words
may have been peculiar to a given dialect, others spread
through adjacent dialects; many slang words and occupational terms were spread through dialect speech generally.
In each dialect area we must imagine a vocabulary, part
Standard English, part dialect, the latter including most
of the occupational terms and most of the slang and

[4] Preface to *A Provincial Glossary*; as quoted in Tucker, *English
Examined*, p. 133.

[5] F. Grose, *Classical Dictionary of the Vulgar Tongue* (ed. Partridge), p. 7.

colloquial words and phrases to do with everyday life in
the area—words associated with physical features, flora,
living conditions, domestic implements, amusements, types
of people, their activities and behaviour.

In the cities, although we may assume a vocabulary of
slang words which were generally current, we must take
account also of various 'specialist' vocabularies, of slang
peculiar to trades and professions, and to certain classes of
criminals. Thus Grose divides his 'vulgar tongue' into two
parts: the first 'the Cant Language, called sometimes Pedlars
French, or St. Giles's Greek', the secret language of a class
of criminals or more generally the slang of criminals,
vagabonds, and prostitutes; and the second, what he calls
'burlesque phrases, quaint allusions, and nick-names for
persons, things, and places',[6] general slang words culled, as
he says, 'from the most classical authorities; such as soldiers
on the long march, seamen at the capstern, ladies disposing
of their fish, and the colloquies of a Gravescend boat'.[7]

It is, of course, unlikely that the equilibrium maintained
in Britain between educated, upper-class usage—that revealed in the prose of the period and safeguarded in
edition after edition of Johnson's *Dictionary*—and the
various regional and social dialects should have been
transported undisturbed to Australia. It would have
needed only a slight shift in the balance, a reduction in
the proportion of cultivated English speakers or an increase in the proportion of speakers of any one regional
or social dialect, for tendencies which had previously been
shared by a minority and kept in check by their relation
to the rest of the speech community to grow and flourish
unchecked by the new pattern of social intercourse. It is
important that the pattern of early Australian English is
seen in this way, not as the beginnings of a new language
but as a reshuffling of an existing English pattern in which
various nuclei—the slang and dialect vocabularies of
London and the industrial Midlands, the slang of seamen
and whalers, the slang of convicts, and the more conserva-

[6] Ibid., p. 7.
[7] Ibid., p. 9.

tive English of the administrators and the military—are set off in a new relationship one against the other.

A reshuffling of this sort involves both gain and loss, the extent to which the various regional and social dialect vocabularies were retained in Australia depending on the proportion of settlers to whom they were familiar and on their utility. We should expect to find a substantial carry-over from English criminal cant—and Vaux's *Vocabulary of the Flash Language,* compiled at Newcastle in 1812, is proof enough that this cant was common to Sydney and London. We should also expect to find an equally substantial carry-over from the regional dialects of words relating to features of the landscape, and to agricultural and pastoral pursuits. But we do not, it being precisely in words of this kind that the vocabulary of the settlers was most deficient. This in itself would suggest what has now been amply proved by the historians, that many of the early settlers were townspeople, and that by far the greater number of the convicts were habitual criminals from the city slums.

Precise information on the origins of the settlers who arrived before 1850 is not easy to find. Returns printed annually from 1839 in the *Votes and Proceedings of the Legislative Council of New South Wales* give the numbers of English and Welsh, Scots and Irish coming in to Australia but no more detailed information. Birth places of immigrants are not recorded and only a very general picture can be gained of an 'amalgam produced by the settlement in the century after 1788 of English and Welsh, Irish and Scots, drawn largely from the "lower half" of the social strata of their countries of origin'.[8]

The number of Irish immigrants is large: roughly 30 per cent of the convicts, 48 per cent of the assisted immigrants who arrived in Australia before 1851, and 33 per cent of the unassisted immigrants were Irish.[9] The proportion of Scots was small—13 per cent of the assisted

---

[8] W. D. Borrie, 'Australia', in O. Handlin and B. Thomas (ed.), *The Positive Contribution by Immigrants,* p. 78.

[9] Ibid., p. 80.

immigrants and 15 per cent of the unassisted immigrants in the period up to 1860. These were mostly of 'middle class, tenant farmer stock', hard working and better educated than the Irish, less likely to influence the 'outlook and songs of the Australian working people'.[10] The numbers and noisiness of the Irish were frequently mentioned by visitors to the colony.[11] It is at first sight surprising that these early Irish settlers, many of whose songs survive, should have made no separate and distinctly Irish contribution to the Australian vocabulary, those words used in Australia which are recorded by Wright as current in Ireland being recorded also in English dialects, particularly that of Lancashire.

One reason for this is that, in a heterogeneous society like that of early New South Wales, no one dialect group would have remained isolated enough to preserve its individuality. The more extravagant features of accent and idiom would probably not have survived the first generation. Thus English visitors to New South Wales comment regularly on 'colonial' speech and manners without suggesting that the influence of any one dialect is noticeably strong.

It is perhaps more important that the most significant population movement in Britain in the early nineteenth century was of impoverished Irish workers to the new factory areas of Lancashire, Yorkshire, and Scotland. Many of these must have subsequently been transported to Sydney as convicts or come out as assisted immigrants, and their speech, as that of a minority group in the English towns, would already have been modified.

The movement of the Irish to England, and the consequent depletion of their dialect vocabulary, is paralleled by a movement of the English rural labouring population into the industrial towns, and there must have been, in the first part of the nineteenth century, a substantial change in the status and distribution of many dialect words. Thus there are some words which were common to parts

[10] Russel Ward, *The Australian Legend*, p. 46.
[11] Ibid., p. 48.

of Ireland and to Lancashire, and a number of dialect words which passed into general currency as slang—in the towns—at much the same time as they were first used in Australia. Examples of these are *to bone,* 'to steal'; *caulker,* 'a drink'; *to cook,* 'to kill'; *corker; dust-up; to hum,* 'to deceive'; *to mag,* 'to talk'; *to nick* and *to nobble,* both meaning 'to steal'; *to peg out,* 'to die'; *purler,* 'a fall'; *scran,* 'food'; *to take a rise out of someone*; and *tootsy,* 'foot'.

Conditions in England were such that this shift in the balance was only to be expected. The continued enclosure of open fields and commons, the decline in importance of domestic or cottage industries, and the growth of the new factory areas all contributed to the displacement of the rural population and the consequent expansion of the towns.

And, as one would expect, the new arrivals tended to come from the surrounding districts rather than from areas further away. Arthur Redford has shown that 'a great proportion of the migrants into Lancashire had come from the surrounding counties' and that

> migration into the other great centres of manufacturing and mining industry showed the same short-distance movement from all neighbouring counties. The woollen towns of the West Riding received much labour from the north and east of Yorkshire, as well as from Lincolnshire. Birmingham and the neighbouring group of towns drew labourers from the rural parts of Staffordshire and Warwickshire, together with considerable numbers from Shropshire on the west and Northamptonshire on the east.[12]

Many of those who migrated to the towns found themselves unemployed, living in the most appalling and overcrowded slums, and forced, sooner or later, to turn to crime for a living; and it is therefore no surprise that the greater number of convicts, and probably the greater number of immigrants to Australia, were townspeople. Some, as the evidence of population movements within the Brit-

[12] A. Redford, *Labour Migration in England, 1800-1850,* pp. 55-6.

ish Isles suggests, were probably first-generation townspeople, with a not very remote rural background,[13] but
even these, like the Irish in Lancashire, had passed through
a time when the pressure would have been on them to
adapt their vocabulary and pronunciation to that of the
townspeople amongst whom they were living, and to
abandon features of their native dialect.

Evidence on the origins of the convicts is more precise.
Governor Hunter, in 1796, had criticized convict settlers
who were 'unfitted for farming by inclination or ability',[14]
an opinion Commissioner Bigge confirmed in 1822:

> A very large proportion of the convicts assigned to the
> settlers, having, in the later periods of the colony
> consisted of the lower classes of labourers from the
> manufacturing districts of Great Britain, or from the
> populous towns, much difficulty has been experienced
> in training them to agricultural labour on their arrival.[15]

Details of trials and other particulars on the convict
indents confirm this view.[16] The counties from which
almost 40 per cent of the male convicts were transported
to New South Wales and Van Diemen's Land were those
with the largest urban concentrations: London, Lancashire, Dublin, Yorkshire, Warwickshire, and Surrey.[17]
Most of those who came from the towns came from the
criminal classes, more than half of them with prior con-
victions.[18] The proportion of convicts from rural areas was
small and, even so, about a third of those tried in rural
areas were vagrants, 'habitual criminals, such as horse-

---

[13] Ward, *The Australian Legend*, p. 20.

[14] Quoted in R. B. Madgwick, *Immigration into Eastern Australia*,
p. 39.

[15] J. T. Bigge, *Report on the Commission of Inquiry into the
State of the Colony of New South Wales*, p. 75.

[16] See C. M. H. Clark, 'The Origins of the Convicts Transported
to Eastern Australia, 1788-1852', *Historical Studies, Australia and
New Zealand*, vol. 7 (1956), no. 26, pp. 121-35 and no. 27, pp. 314-27;
and L. L. Robson, *The Convict Settlers of Australia*.

[17] Robson, *The Convict Settlers of Australia*, p. 18.

[18] Ibid., p. 143.

stealers and housebreakers' and mendicants, who 'travelled the country from town to town and from fair to fair in search of dishonest gain'.[19]

Approximately 168,000 convicts were transported to Australia before transportation ceased in 1868.[20] Their language, like that of many of the free settlers, would largely have been the common or vulgar language of the towns, characterized by a large proportion of general slang words, and 'specialist' slang of the criminal classes. The balance of British English, where a refined standard usage was set off against both the vulgar language of the towns and the variety of regional dialects, was changed: the level of refined usage continued in much the same relation to the others as it had in British English, but the importance of the regional vocabularies decreased and that of the vulgar levels of usage increased.

The reduced importance of the regional vocabularies is in some ways more important than the increase in the vulgar levels. The slang vocabulary was extensive and a good proportion of it survived transplanting, but it was a vocabulary of limited usefulness in the colony. The reduction in the regional vocabularies of words associated with sheep husbandry and agriculture, along with the loss of words from the standard vocabulary for physical features of the landscape, made necessary an enormous expansion in this direction. 'The rich variety of traditional technical words',[21] lost to settlers from the towns, was inevitably replaced by a basic vocabulary of general terms, a vocabulary which was then expanded by the normal means of word-formation in English, extension in meaning, composition, and derivation.

Sir Keith Hancock has lamented the Australian's rejection, almost at a blow, of 'the beautiful names of an intimate countryside—fields and meadows, woods, copse, spinney and thicket, dale, glen, vale and coomb, brook,

[19] Ibid., p. 24.
[20] C. M. H. Clark, *A Short History of Australia*, p. 117.
[21] A. G. Mitchell, *Australian Accent*, p. 25.

stream and rivulet, inn and village'.[22] Words of this sort
survived, as one might expect, in the poetry of Harpur
and Kendall, but they are used also with surprising frequency by writers like Alexander Harris: *woods* beside
bush, *flock* or *herd* beside *mob*, *fold* beside *yard*, *sheep
walk* beside *run*, *brook* beside *creek*, *cottage* beside *hut*,
and so on. Sometimes Harris seeks to achieve a particular
effect, but usually there is no apparent reason for the
choice, and it is impossible to tell whether, writing for an
English audience, he unconsciously oscillated between the
two levels of usage or whether his usage reflects actual
Australian usage at a time when an educated speaker could
still choose between the two sets of terms. He did not
apparently feel that it was inappropriate to apply the
traditional words to the Australian landscape and conditions, so we can assume, therefore, that these words
dropped out of general use in Australia because, as part
of provincial usage or as part of a cultivated, literary
usage, they were unfamiliar to many of the settlers. It is
the gap left in the vocabulary that is important, however,
and it is through an examination of the ways in which
this gap was filled that the distinguishing characteristics
of Australian English are revealed.

The dialect words that survive in Australian English,
then, are mostly those words which would have had a
place in the colloquial usage in both the country and the
city; and, where they come from rural as opposed to urban
areas, they are mostly from dialect areas adjacent to the
growing industrial towns. There are a few words associated
with animals and farming, a few names for topographical
features and, coming into use during the 1850s, a few
mining terms, but most of the survivals in the following
lists could have been used as commonly in the towns as in
the rural areas. As parts of occupational vocabularies, the
mining terms and the words associated with animal husbandry have changed little in meaning and their area of
application has remained much the same. But many of
the other words, moving into general colloquial speech or

[22] W. K. Hancock, *Australia*, p. 242.

E

slang, at the vulgar rather than the cultivated level, have changed their meanings slightly or acquired wider areas of application.[23]

1   LOUD TALK, DRINKING, GAMBLING, AND TRICKERY

barney	long-sleever
barrack	ready-up
bender	school
blow	shivoo
carney	shout
chiack	stonker
cross	taws
fakement	

Some of these words are no longer current. *Carney*, used as a verb, meaning 'to coax, flatter, or wheedle', or as a noun, meaning 'cajolery or flattery', was fairly widely distributed in the midland and southern dialects of England and was in use in Australia before 1850. *Cross*, meaning 'wrong', passed into English slang at the end of the eighteenth century and was recorded as criminal cant by Vaux in 1812 (see p. 12 above). Alexander Harris used it frequently, as an adjective meaning 'illegally acquired' or in the phrase *on the cross*, meaning 'dishonestly', and both usages are fairly common in Boldrewood's novels in the latter part of the century. *Fakement*, similarly, passed from regional dialect speech into slang: a Devonshire word for 'muddle or confusion', it came to mean a 'contrivance or dodge', in which sense it was used in the second half of the century in Australia. *To ready-up*, meaning 'to swindle' or 'to manipulate in an improper way', became more generally current at the end of the century and is still in use.

[23] Information on the English use of dialect words is almost always from Wright's *English Dialect Dictionary*. There are obvious disadvantages in using a dictionary compiled at the end of the nineteenth century. Wright drew his material from earlier glossaries and from correspondents and the status and distribution of some dialect words changed greatly during the century under consideration. See also the *Oxford English Dictionary* and the *Scottish National Dictionary*.

Barney, barrack, blow, and *chiack* are all words associated with loud talk, noise, and arguments. *Barney,* used as a noun meaning 'dispute or altercation' or a verb meaning 'to argue', retains its original dialect sense, as does *to blow,* meaning 'to boast'. *Chiack* (*chyack,* or *chi-hike*), on the other hand, has shifted away from its earlier sense. Hotten described it as 'a hurrah, a good word, or hearty praise; [a] term used by *costermongers* who assist the sale of each other's goods by a little friendly although noisy commendation',[24] and, in Australian use, it has come to mean 'to cheek' or 'to chaff', having a more general application. C. R. Read, in *What I Heard, Saw, and Did at the Australian Gold Fields,* uses it to describe the miners' treatment of police seeking to inspect licences;[25] thereafter, it is used mostly of men joking amongst themselves.

Just as an Aboriginal origin has been suggested for *chiack,* so one has for *barrack.* In the forties and fifties a Victorian Aboriginal negative, *borak,* became current in Aboriginal pidgin, and it is from this that the *Oxford English Dictionary,* following Morris, derives *barrack.* But there is no connection between the two words. Nor is there any truth in the suggestion that

the word was first coined in Melbourne owing to the proficiency of roaring encouragement and howling abuse displayed by the supporters of a football team that had its habitat near some artillery barracks.[26]

To barrack for someone, meaning 'to support someone vociferously against others' is most probably derived from the Northern Irish word meaning 'to brag, to be boastful of one's fighting powers'. In Australian English it refers mostly to support given at a sporting fixture, support which may range from the 'coarse language used by roughs in applauding their party in a contest'[27] to the much quieter support implied by the familiar greeting of spectators

24 J. C. Hotten, *Dictionary of Modern Slang, Cant, and Vulgar Words.*
25 Read's spelling (p. 148) is *skyhacking.*
26 *Bulletin,* 8 February 1933, p. 11.
27 Cornelius Crowe, *Australian Slang Dictionary.*

'Who are you barracking for?' Without the preposition, *to barrack* has come more to mean 'to criticize or to chaff'.

Bender, long-sleever, shivoo, and *shout* are all words related to drink and drinking. *Bender,* meaning 'a drinking frolic or spree' and most commonly used in the phrase *to go on a bender,* is dialectal in origin and found in both the United States and Australia. *Long-sleever,* slang for a tall beer-glass, was current at the end of the century and is presumably derived from *sleever,* a word recorded by the *English Dialect Dictionary* in Monmouthshire for 'a glass of beer containing more than half a pint but less than a full pint'.

Probably misled by Alexander Harris's elegant spelling *shiveau,*[28] Baker derived *shivoo* from the French *chez vous,*[29] but it again is of dialectal origin, the *English Dialect Dictionary* recording *sheevo* or *shevo* in Yorkshire and Cornwall with the sense 'a disturbance, row or shindy'. There are, similarly, conflicting theories about the origin of *shout.* Morris suggested that the word was derived from the practice of the successful digger calling others to drink at his expense; from the necessity, in a crowded and noisy bar, of having to shout for the waiter; or from the expression *to pay the shot.* Baker thought that 'it was obviously derived from shouting for attention at a bar'.[30] But the word *shot,* meaning 'a payment, a bill, a share of a reckoning', was widely current in English and Scottish dialect speech, and it seems a short step from one usage recorded by the *English Dialect Dictionary* in Shropshire —'Now, chaps, whad' nee a to drink—ale or short [spirits]? —an' I'll stand shot'—to the simple Australian 'My shout'. Nor is it hard to see how, once other uses of *shot,* meaning 'a share of the reckoning' were forgotten, the apparent connection with *shout* should lead to the new form, and to the formation of a verb.

School, stonker, and *taws* are all dialect words used in games or gambling. *School* was used in English slang to mean 'a company of thieves or beggars working together';

[28] *The Emigrant Family,* vol. 1, p. 114.
[29] *The Australian Language,* p. 168.
[30] Ibid., p. 170.

but the Australian usage seems to be distinct from this. Vaux defined *school* as 'a party of persons met together for the purpose of gambling', a Northumberland usage, and it is in this sense that the word has continued to be used in Australia. Both *stonker* and *taws* are terms borrowed from the game of marbles. *Taw*, in dialect English, may mean 'a marble', 'a game of marbles', or 'the mark from which marbles are shot' (and, by extension, 'the mark or line from which runners, or leapers, or players in any game start'.) It is this last meaning which has given rise to the Australian use of the word, usually in the expressions *back to taws*, 'back to scratch, back to the beginning', and *to start off from taws*. *Stonk* was used in Scotland and the English Midlands for 'the stake in a game, especially a game of marbles'. It is probable that the Australian use of *to stonker*, meaning 'to destroy, thwart, vanquish, put out of action', and of the past participle *stonkered*, meaning 'beaten' (by a wide variety of things which may include an opponent's blow, and excessive food or drink) derive from this.

2   PEOPLE, CHARACTERISTICS OF PEOPLE

cobber	rouseabout
dubersome	sheila
guiver	smarmy
jonnick	smoodger
knockabout	snitchy
larrikin	sorny
nark	tinny
pommy	wowser
roughie	

Here, again, there are some words which are now obsolete. *Dubersome*, found in Australian English in the latter part of the century, was widely used in dialect speech in the sense of 'doubtful, dubious'. *Guiver*, meaning 'plausible talk, ingratiating behaviour designed to flatter and deceive', and in use in the sixties, is probably related to dialectal *givour*, 'greedy', or *guyvisome*, 'foolish'. It is now little used, if not obsolete, as is *jonnick* (or *jannock*), meaning 'fair, honest, straightforward'.

Larrikin, on the other hand, has not only become more widely used in Australia than it was in Britain, but has actually been borrowed back and brought into more general currency in England. Various etymologies have again been proposed for this word, the most popular that reported by Morris, quoting a W. H. Whelan in the Melbourne *Argus*:

> Being clerk of the City Court, I know that the word originated in the very Irish and amusing way in which the then well-known Sergeant Dalton pronounced the word larking in respect to the conduct of 'Tommy the Nut', a rowdy of the period, and others of both sexes in Stephen (now Exhibition) Street.
>
> Your representative at the Court, the witty and clever 'Billy' O'Hea, who, alas! died too early, took advantage of the appropriate sound of the word to apply it to rowdyism in general, and, next time Dalton repeated the phrase, changed the word from verb to noun, where it still remains, anything to the contrary notwithstanding. I speak of what I do know, for O'Hea drew my attention to the matter at the time, and, if I mistake not, a reference to your files would show that it was first in the 'Argus' the word appeared in print.[31]

The editors of the *Argus* stood firmly behind Whelan.

Others have suggested that the word was 'thieves' English, promoted . . . into ordinary Australian English' and made up of *leary*, 'knowing', and *kinchen* or *kid*, 'youngster'; or that it was derived from French *larron*, 'a thief', and *kid*.[32] In the same year that Morris was considering these theories Joshua Lake, editing the Australasian Supplement to *Webster's Dictionary*, first suggested the word's dialectal origin: and, in confirmation of this, it is with the basic Australian meaning, 'a mischievous or frolicsome youth', that the *English Dialect Dictionary* records *larrikin* in Warwickshire and Worcestershire.

Just as larrikin was once attributed to a journalist's

[31] Morris, *Austral English*.
[32] Ibid.

inventiveness so John Norton, editor of *Truth* during the 1890s, is reputed to have coined *wowser*. Norton himself had no hesitation in claiming credit for the word's invention:

> 'Everyone knows right well what the word Wowser really means and what a Wowser is', he wrote. 'Even among sectarian savages and smellfull saints of the dirty dickeys, soiled shirts, stale singlets, and stinking socks, the real meaning of the word Wowser is as well known as the meanings of such words and phrases as larrikin and hooligan, bludger and wop, Johnny Woodser, Johnny Warder, Dicken, "I don't think", and "I should smile".
>
> 'I invented the word myself. I was the first man publicly to use the word. I first gave it public utterance in the City Council, when I applied it to Alderman Waterhouse, whom I referred to . . . as the white, woolly, weary, watery, word-wasting wowser from Waverley.
>
> 'I am proud of my invention. The fabrication of such a word—absolutely absent from, but absolutely required in our local vernacular, until I invented it—was a stroke of genius, done on the spur of the moment, impromptu, the result of divine or diabolical inspiration. Therefore "Palmam Qui Meruit Ferat"—the motto of Lord Nelson, let it be the motto of John Norton . . . for the purpose of establishing his claim to immortal glory as the inventor of the word Wowser.
>
> 'To my humble self—to me, John Norton, alone belongs the sole undivided glory and renown of inventing a word, a single, simple word, that does at once describe, deride, and denounce that numerous, noxious, pestilent, puritanical, kill-joy push—the whole blasphemous, wire-whiskered brood.'[33]

It may be that Norton gave *wowser* its early currency in Australian English, but his claim to have invented the word is hardly warranted in view of the widespread dialectal use of *to wow*, meaning 'to mew as a cat, howl or bark as a dog, wail, to whine, grumble, complain'. Like *larrikin*, *wowser* did, at any rate, achieve general currency

[33] Cyril Pearl, *Wild Men of Sydney*, pp. 113-14.

in Australia, since when it has been borrowed into British and American English as a useful and expressive name for any 'ineffably pious person who mistakes this world for a penitentiary and himself for a warder'.[34]

Knockabout, 'an odd-job man' or 'handyman', and *rouse-about*, 'a station-hand who looks after the odd jobs' are both dialect words which have undergone a similar change in meaning. *Knockabout* is a word from Yorkshire and the Midlands which meant 'wanderer', *rouseabout* a word from the southern English dialects which was used of 'a restless creature, never easy at home, but roaming from place to place'.[35] *Roughie*, meaning 'a coarsely made, bullying fellow' was used in both Scotland and Ireland, *nark* (as a verb meaning 'to annoy' or as a noun, 'the source of the annoyance') widely through the Midlands and the north of England. *Sheila*, recorded by Crowe in 1895 as *shaler*,[36] is probably Irish; *smarmy*, meaning 'falsely polite, smooth-tongued', *snitchy*, meaning 'cross, ill-tempered, snappy, disdainful', *soony* or *sorny*, meaning 'sentimental', and *tinny*, meaning 'lucky', dialect words which, with slight changes in meaning, have had a long history in Australian colloquial speech. *Smoodge* (or *smooge*), whence *smoodger*, would seem to be derived from one of two dialect verbs, *smoodge*, meaning 'to covet, long for, to sidle up to, to beg in a sneaking way', and *smouch*, 'to kiss', especially 'to kiss loudly or in a dirty, slobbering manner'.

Cobber and *pommy* are, again, widely used words with hotly disputed etymologies. It has been suggested that *cobber* is derived from Yiddish *chuver*, 'a comrade, pal or buddy'[37] but, when there is no clear evidence one way or another, it seems less probable that the word was borrowed from the language of a small immigrant minority than

[34] C. J. Dennis, *Backblock Ballads and Other Verses*, Glossary.
[35] *Oxford English Dictionary*.
[36] *Australian Slang Dictionary*.
[37] R. J. Menner, 'The Australian Language', *American Speech*, vol. 21 (1946), p. 120; and D. O'Meara, 'Australian "Cobber"', *American Speech*, vol. 21 (1946), p. 273.

that it was a survival or derivative of any one of several known dialectal forms, the most likely being the verb, *to cob*, 'to take a liking to anyone', recorded in Suffolk.

The derivation of *pommy* remains a mystery. Partridge suggests several possibilities: that it is a corruption of *Tommy* or of *pom pom*; that it is a blend of *jimmy*, 'a silly person' (used in Australia of immigrants) and *Tommy*; that it is an abbreviation of *Pomeranian*, 'a very superior sort of "dawg" '; that it is derived from *immigrant* or *jimmy-grant*, and influenced by *pomegranate* because of the traditional ruddiness of the Englishman's cheeks.[38] Others have suggested that it is derived from *Pompey*, a slang term for Portsmouth, or that it is from *pommé*, a Breton colloquialism for 'complete, downright, out and out', imported by Cornish miners.[39]

Pommy is first recorded in Australian English during World War I, when it gives every appearance of being generally established, and Partridge asserts that it was in use before then. It may, like *jimmy*, have been in colloquial use during the latter part of the nineteenth century. It is generally derogatory in its connotations and one possibility, no more unlikely than those already suggested, is that it is derived from *pom*, *pommy*, or *pummy*, variant forms of *pomace*, a word used in several of the southern English dialects of 'apples crushed into a pulp in preparation for the making of cider'. *All of a pom*, or *all of a pommy* was a phrase used to describe squashy or over-ripe fruit, and the word seems to have been used figuratively of other things which were messy or unpleasant. Other, and more fanciful, derivations will undoubtedly be produced but, until the early history of the word in Australia is more fully documented, one can do little more than guess at the probable origin.

[38] Eric Partridge, *Dictionary of Slang and Unconventional English*, 4th ed.

[39] D. Waymouth, *The Times*, 27 December 1963. Another suggestion (*Time*, 23 July 1965, p. 4) is that it is formed from the initial letters of *Prisoner of Mother England*; but this argues a much longer history in Australian English than the word is known to have.

3 INTENSIVES; EXPRESSIONS FOR GREAT SIZE

boomer	jimbang
buster	ringer
flaming	sollicker

The earliest of these to be found in use in Australia is *boomer*, a Warwickshire word meaning 'anything very large of its kind'. It occurs from the thirties on as the popular name for a large kangaroo, and is sometimes spelt *boomah* because of its supposed Aboriginal origin. But there are instances of *boomer* being used as an expression of great size in other contexts[40]—the most familiar being as a description of a large wave—and it is a reasonable assumption that behind these lies the continued collo-quial use of the dialect word. *Buster* was similarly used in the southern dialects of England, and it is most probably from this generalized use that the two particularized Australian meanings have developed: from the fifties *buster* was used, mostly in the expression *southerly buster*, to describe a sudden and violent wind;[41] and, in the latter part of the century, it came also to mean 'a heavy fall'.

Ringer, again, is a Yorkshire word with a fairly general meaning, used originally of 'anything superlatively good'. In Australia it has become a part of shearing slang, used specifically of the fastest shearer in the shed. The verb *to ring* is used in the same context and, perhaps misled by this, some commentators have sought the origin of the word in the quoits expression meaning 'a quoit which rings the peg' or in the widely used phrase *to run rings around*.[42] But the word is recorded in Australia in its more general application,[43] so there seems little justification for seeking another derivation.

Boomer, *buster*, and *ringer* survived in Australian Eng-lish because, in their new senses, they met specific needs in the vocabulary. *Sollicker*, derived from a Yorkshire word *sollock*, meaning 'impetus' or 'force', met no such need,

[40] See Baker, *The Australian Language*, pp. 213, 277.
[41] G. C. Mundy, *Our Antipodes*, vol. 1, p. 83.
[42] See quotations in Morris, *Austral English*.
[43] Ibid.

was current for a time about the turn of the century, but
seems now to be obsolete. The two intensives *jimbang*
(commonly shortened to *bang*) and *flaming* (as in that
most picturesque of Australianisms, *stone the flaming
crows!*) both became part of the colloquial vocabulary in
the latter part of the century and are still in use.

4 EFFORT OR MOVEMENT

bore	lick
buck	scratch
hump	sling

These are mostly straightforward examples of words
which survive from the regional dialects with little or no
change in their meanings. *To bore* was used in Somerset
of a horse, meaning 'to rush straight on with the head
down and the bit between his teeth'. Boldrewood used the
word with the same sense,[44] and it has subsequently
developed a wider area of application in colloquial speech,
being used of anyone or anything (a queue-crasher or foot-
baller, for instance) who rushes or pushes blindly forward.
To hump, meaning 'to shoulder and carry something'
(most commonly a *bluey*); *to lick*, meaning 'to travel fast'
and common in the expressions *as hard as one can lick* or,
as a noun, *to go at a good lick*; *to scratch*, meaning again
'to travel fast'; and *to sling*, meaning 'to walk with long
or swinging strides', are all equally certainly dialect words,
despite Baker's assertion that *scratch* was an invention of
Boldrewood's.[45]

But the origin of the verb *to buck*, from which *buck-
jump* and *buckjumper* were subsequently formed, is less
sure. *Buck* is current in the United States and New Zealand, probably as a borrowing from Australian English,
and in South African English, where Pettman derives it
from Dutch *bokken maken*, 'to cut capers', and records it
in use in the 1850s.[46] This is, of course, a possibility, but

[44] *Robbery Under Arms*, p. 63.
[45] *The Australian Language*, p. 300.
[46] *Africanderisms*.

buck is recorded in Australian English in 1848;[47] *buck-jump* in 1852.[48] Both seem to have been in fairly common use from that time, which suggests a longer period of Australian use than the evidence at present available indicates. There are, moreover, several English dialect words from which the Australian usage might have been derived, particularly *to boke*, used generally with the meaning of 'to thrust', but also, of horses, meaning 'to shy'; it seems more likely that one of these, or a related form, was carried into Australian English than that a word newly coined in South Africa was borrowed and so quickly became current.

5   DOMESTIC FEATURES, FOODS, CLOTHING

billy	jumper
bowyangs	kellick
clobber	kip
damper	skillion
dodger	swag
dolly	tucker

Like so many of the words considered in this chapter *billy* has remained a puzzle to the etymologist. The *Oxford English Dictionary*, following Morris, derives the word from the proper name *William*, the usage being similar to that of *Jenny* in *Spinning Jenny*. Baker derives *billy* from Aboriginal *billa*, 'water',[49] and another suggested derivation is recorded by Morris and *Webster's*:

> *Billy* is shortened from *billycan*, which is said to be bully-can (sc. Fr. *bouilli*). In the early days 'boeuf bouilli' was a common label on tins of preserved meat in ship's stores. These tins, called 'bully-tins', were used by diggers and others as the modern billy is.[50]

None of these is very likely: *billy* preceded *billycan* by many years and there is no evidence of the Aboriginal

---

[47] *Our Antipodes*, vol. 1, p. 248 (quoting a statement written in 1848).

[48] W. Howitt, *Land, Labour and Gold*, vol. 1, p. 43.

[49] *The Australian Language*, p. 83.

[50] *Austral English*.

pidgin use of *billa*, meaning 'water', which one would expect to precede the sort of transference Baker suggests. There are, however, two Scottish dialect words, *bally*, meaning 'milk pail', recorded by the *English Dialect Dictionary* and the *Scottish National Dictionary*, and *billypot*, 'a cooking utensil', recorded by the *Scottish National Dictionary*, which may be related to, if not actually the source of, the word which, in Australian English, Howitt referred to as 'a tin kettle or billy, as the diggers call it'.[51]

Dolly, a goldmining term for 'an instrument used by diggers for dividing and mixing the tough clay or cement with water in the puddling tub',[52] is derived from a widely used dialect name for a similar contrivance for washing clothes; *kelk*, whence *kellick* or *killick*, a Cumberland and Yorkshire word for 'a large detached stone', used in Australia by fishermen and referring to 'a weight, often a stone, tied to a rope for mooring a boat'. *Kip*, 'the small flat piece of board with which the pennies are spun in two-up', is also most probably of dialectal origin. *Skillion*, or *skilling* as it was spelt in Australian English before about 1840, was fairly widely used in Southern English dialects for a 'lean-to' or 'outhouse'. According to Acland it was used in New Zealand in the nineteenth century of 'the sheep-holding part of a woolshed';[53] but in Australia it has always referred to a lean-to used as a store room or bedroom and attached to the hut or house;[54] subsequently it has come to be used of a type of roof and also of a headland near Terrigal, New South Wales.

Bowyangs, in Australia 'pieces of string, or anything tieable, commonly used by labourers to hitch up trousers under the knees',[55] is derived from a Lincolnshire word meaning 'leather leggings'; *jumper*, a widely used dialect word for 'a fisherman's jersey, a short, loose coat, a blue

---

[51] *Land, Labour and Gold*, vol. 1, p. 195.

[52] R. B. Smyth, *Goldfields of Victoria*, p. 609.

[53] Acland, 'A Sheep Station Glossary'.

[54] See *Letters of Rev. Richard Johnson*, 26 August 1799; *H.R.A.*, vol. xiv, p. 47; *Port Phillip Gazette*, 19 August 1843, p. 1.

[55] *Bulletin*, 4 October 1896 (Red Page).

serge shirt'. Baker claims it as 'almost certainly an Australian invention',[56] but it comes into Australian during the goldrush period with exactly the sense it had in English dialectal usage and was presumably borrowed from immigrant miners or seamen. Howitt describes the digger's uniform in some detail:

> As for the generality of the men, they are, to look at, as rude fellows as you ever saw. They beat your navvies at home all to nothing. They are generally rigged out in strong fustian trousers, and stout shoes or boots; a blouse or, cloth shirt, which they call a 'jumper', tucked into their trousers,—sometimes blue, often scarlet, and as often of great tawdry stripes of red and white, and blue and white, and, in fact, of all sorts of strange and flaming colours. They almost all wear the dirty battered cabbage-tree hat, and have grim beards, and look as if they never washed.[57]

And Mossman and Banister, in 1853, refer to gold-diggers, 'clad in their peculiar plaid or checquered jumper'.[58]

The digger's clothing, odds and ends of possessions, and bedding, rolled together, made up a *swag*. Vaux, in 1812, recorded *swag* as a criminal cant word for stolen 'wearing-apparel, linen, piece-goods, etc.' as distinguished from plate or jewellery (see p. 12 above), and the later Australian use seems to be derived either from this or from the regional dialect use of the word for 'a bag or burden'. From it are derived the use of *swag* as a verb, and the nouns *swagger*, *swaggie*, *swagman*, and *swagsman*.

Rolling a swag is, by now, a lost art, and Henry Lawson's scrupulous instructions are worth remembering for this reason:

> The swag is usually composed of a tent 'fly' or strip of calico (a cover for the swag and a shelter in bad weather —in New Zealand it is oilcloth or waterproof twill), a couple of blankets, blue by custom and preference, as that colour shows the dirt less than any other (hence the

---

[56] *The Australian Language*, p. 182.
[57] *Land, Labour and Gold*, vol. 1, p. 113.
[58] S. Mossman and T. Banister, *Australia Visited and Revisited*, p. 33.

name 'bluey' for swag), and the core is composed of spare clothing and small personal effects. To make or 'roll up' your swag: lay the fly or strip of calico on the ground, blueys on top of it; across one end, with eighteen inches or so to spare, lay your spare trousers and shirt, folded, light boots tied together by the laces toe to heel, books, bundles of old letters, portraits, or whatever little knick-knacks you have or care to carry, bag of needles, thread, pen and ink, spare patches for your pants, and bootlaces. Lay or arrange the pile so that it will roll evenly with the swag (some pack the lot in an old pillowslip or canvas bag), take a fold over of blanket and calico the whole length on each side, so as to reduce the width of the swag to, say, three feet, throw the spare end, with an inward fold, over the little pile of belongings, and then roll the whole to the other end, using your knees and judgement to make the swag tight, compact and artistic; when within eighteen inches of the loose end take an inward fold in that, and bring it up against the body of the swag . . . Fasten the swag with three or four straps . . . To the top strap, for the swag is carried . . . in a more or less vertical position—to the top strap, and lowest, or lowest but one, fasten the ends of the shoulder strap (usually a towel is preferred as being softer to the shoulder), your coat being carried outside the swag at the back, under the straps . . . The weight of the swag varies from the tight rouseabout's swag, containing one blanket and a clean shirt, to the 'royal Alfred', with tent and all complete, and weighing part of a ton.[59]

Clobber, similarly, though it comes into Australian English much later than *swag*, probably had a dialect origin. The *English Dialect Dictionary* records *clubbered up*, 'dressed up', in Kent, and at the end of the century, at much the same time as it is found in Australian English, *clobber* moved into general British slang.

Several Australian words for food or foods are dialectal in origin, notably the generic term for food, *tucker*, which is derived from the widespread regional use of *tuck*, used both as a verb and as a noun, and which gives rise in

[59] 'The Romance of the Swag', in *Prose Works of Henry Lawson*, pp. 474-5.

Australian English to a number of compounds, the most
familiar of which are *tuckerbag* and *tuckerbox*. *Dodger*,
used in Australia of a loaf of bread and in the United
States of a hard-baked corn-cake, is derived from a dialect
word meaning 'a large cut or slice of food', and *damper*,
'the universal bread of the bush'[60] from a Lancashire word
for a light snack between meals.

6   ANIMAL   HUSBANDRY,   FARMING,   LANDSCAPE   FEATURES,
    TIMBER

back o' beyond	poddy
bail	poley
chook	pug
claypan	run
cracker	shanghai
dee	snig
dinkum	soak
fall	sowl
mudfat	staggering bob
paddock	waterhole

Most of these are occupational words and their meanings
in Australia are little different from those in England.
Thus *cracker* means 'the small cord at the end of a whip
which causes it to crack', *dee*, 'an iron shaped like the
letter D', *pug*, 'well pounded clay for building walls'. *To
fall*, meaning 'to cut down', was used by timber-getters
instead of the Standard English, *to fell*; and *to snig*, another timber usage, meant 'to drag a heavy load by means
of ropes or chains, to draw timber out of a wood without
a cart'.

Mudfat was a Northern Irish word used of stock which
meant 'very fat'; *staggering bob* a widespread dialect
phrase used either of a very young calf which has not yet
found its legs or of the veal from such a calf. *Poddy*, used
mostly of handfed calves, means 'fat' or 'pot-bellied', *poley*,
'a hornless cow or ox'. *Claypan*, recorded in Australian
English in the sixties,[61] seems to be of Cornish origin, *soak*,

---

[60] Howitt, *Land, Labour and Gold*, vol. 1, p. 117.
[61] J. M. Sturt, 'Diary', 3 May 1860: an extract from an undated
South Australian Advertiser.

for 'a spot of marshy or depressed ground from which a spring rises', and *waterhole* both also from regional dialect vocabularies. *Back o' beyond,* presumably the model for colloquial expressions like *back o' Bourke* and *back of the black stump,* is recorded by the *English Dialect Dictionary* in midland and northern English dialects.

But a few of these underwent a change of meaning. *Chook,* for instance, is derived from *chook* or *chookey,* a word used in some southern dialects as 'a call to pigs, or occasionally to poultry'[62] and *to sool,* or *to sowl,* was a widespread dialect word meaning 'to pull by ears, to pull about roughly, to attack fiercely'. As early as 1849 Harris was using it in its present Australian sense, as a call to dogs to set on someone or something.[63] *Shanghai,* first recorded in the sense of 'catapult' in Australia in the sixties, is probably derived from a Scottish word, *shangy,* meaning 'a stick cleft at one end for putting on a dog's tail'.

Bail, as the name for 'a frame to which cows are tied in byres', came into Australian use in the forties.[64] This was the meaning it had in several English dialects, where it was also used as a verb, meaning 'to tie up, fasten' or 'to command to stand still'. And, as an imperative, it was applied in Australia from the forties on as freely to Christians as to cows,[65] as Boldrewood explained:

One of the young cows was a bit strange with me, so I had to shake a stick at her and sing-out 'Bail up' pretty rough before she'd put her head in . . . It was a rum go, wasn't it? The same talk for cows and Christians. That's how things get stuck into the talk in a new country. Some old hand like father, as had been assigned to a dairy settler and spent all his mornings in the cowyard, had taken to the bush and tried his hand at sticking up people. When they came near enough of course he'd pop out from behind a tree or a rock, with his old musket or a pair of pistols, and when he wanted 'em to

[62] See Howitt, *Land, Labour and Gold,* vol. 2, p. 139-40.
[63] *The Emigrant Family,* vol. 1, p. 286.
[64] Harris, *Settlers and Convicts,* p. 159.
[65] See D. Stewart and N. Keesing (ed.), *Old Bush Songs and Rhymes of Colonial Times,* p. 53.

F

stop 'Bail up d—— yer', would come a deal quicker, and more natural-like to his tongue than 'Stand!'[66]

Paddock and *run* are both dialect words which, in Australia, are used of much larger areas than in England, and the meaning of *run* has been both simplified and generalized. The *English Dialect Dictionary* recorded *run* in Perth and in East Yorkshire with the meaning 'a stretch of pasturage' or 'the right of pasturing a beast in common pasture', but in Australian English it refers simply to 'a large open stretch of land occupied by a settler for grazing stock'. It is found in Australia as early as 1804;[67] by the thirties it was in wide use and has given rise to a number of compounds: *back run, cattle run, sheep run,* and *stock run*. By this time, it is interesting to note, another English word used by the settlers, *sheep walk,* is becoming increasingly rare.

In all early quotations a *run* is a tract of unfenced land used for grazing sheep or cattle; today it is a tract of land used for grazing sheep or cattle, it may be fenced or unfenced, and it may make up the whole of a station or only part of it. Acland records a variety of uses of the word in New Zealand and these may be of some help in pinning down the sense meant in a particular usage:

1) The country held under a particular lease or pastoral licence.
2) A group of *runs* held by one owner, or in one station. The whole area is spoken of as a *run*.
3) Leasehold as opposed to freehold.
4) Open as opposed to fenced country; 'out on the *run*', i.e. not in any of the paddocks.
5) Adjective. *Run* sheep, *run* cattle, as opposed to paddock sheep or milking cows and hand-reared calves.
6) As equivalent to *station* . . . now uncommon.
7) A block of country, a division of a *run,* e.g., *ewe run, upper run*. This sense was always rare, but is still in use on some stations.[68]

[66] *Robbery Under Arms*, p. 368.
[67] *Sydney Gazette*, 12 February 1804, p. 3.
[68] *Sheep Station Glossary*.

The word which has perhaps come to have the fullest associations with Australia is *dinkum*. This is recorded by the *English Dialect Dictionary* in two senses, both of which are used in Australia during the nineteenth century: 'work' or 'a due share of work' as in the phrase 'an hour's hard dinkum',[69] a sense which is now obsolete; and, in the expression *fair dinkum*, 'fair play', from which is derived the Australian use of *dinkum* as an adjective, an adverb, and a noun, with the connotations of 'genuine, honest, and fair'. A number of variant forms like *dinky* and *dinky-di*, are found this century, as well as fixed phrases, like *dinkum article, dinkum oil, square dinkum,* and *honest to dinkum,* all of which testify to the word's popularity and widespread use.

7 MINING

bottom	mullock
buddle	nugget
captain	sprag
crib	stuff
darg	tailings
fossick	

These words, like some of those in the preceding group, are mostly technical or semi-technical words, used in Australia in the same context as they were in England and remaining unchanged in meaning. All, naturally enough, come into use during the fifties and sixties. Thus *bottom,* recorded in Northumberland with the meaning 'the floor of a mine' is used by Australian miners to refer to 'the bedrock'. As R. B. Smyth writes:

> When a shaft reaches the bed-rock, the gold obtained from off the bottom of the shaft is said to be the prospect from off the bottom.[70]

It is also used, both in England and Australia, as a verb, meaning 'to reach the bedrock'. A *buddle* was 'a machine

[69] *Robbery Under Arms,* vol. 1, p. 5 (as quoted in the *English Dialect Dictionary*).
[70] *Goldfields of Victoria,* p. 605.

somewhat similar in construction and use' to a puddling machine, 'used in alluvial mining for extracting gold from sludge, and in quartz mining for separating pyrites from tailings'.[71] *Sprag* meant 'a short prop of timber, used to support the roof of a mine while the pitmen are at work under-cutting'; *stuff*, probably of Cornish origin, was used of ore, or of dirt containing gold; and *tailings* (also Cornish), 'waste', 'the detritus carried off by water from a crushing machine or any gold-washing apparatus'.[72]

Others, not names of implements or processes, were nonetheless peculiar to the vocabulary of miners. Thus the Cornish use of *captain* for 'the superintendent of a mine' carried over into Australian usage, as did *crib*, a word for 'food, something eaten between meals', and *darg*, an Old English word surviving in dialect speech and borrowed from the vocabulary of coalminers, meaning either 'a day's work' or 'the amount of work done in the day'. *Darg* has since become more generally current in colloquial speech.

Fossick and *mullock* were both words used in dialect vocabularies with fairly general meanings which, in Australian usage, were narrowed as the words became current predominantly in the context of goldmining. *To fossick*, a Cornish verb, meant 'to search, or rummage about for anything', and was early current on the Australian gold-fields, giving rise to the derivatives *fossicker* and *fossicking*. Morris distinguished four Australian meanings of the verb: 'to pick out gold' (1852); 'to dig for gold on abandoned claims or in waste-heaps' (1865); 'to search for gold generally, even by stealing' (1861); and 'to search about for anything, to rummage' (1870); but it is unlikely that the first three of these meanings were felt to be distinct from one another, and better perhaps to emphasize the common element of meaning, defining *to fossick* as 'to search for gold in a desultory fashion, usually in abandoned claims, sometimes dishonestly in occupied claims'. Probably because of the frequency with which it was used in descriptions of the goldfields, the word has been given a new lease of life and, in its more general sense, is now widely

[71] Ibid.
[72] Ibid., p. 623.

current in both British and Australian usage. *Mullock*, although it has never been as well known, has followed the same course. Generally current in regional dialects as a synonym for 'rubbish', 'waste', or 'rubble', it came into use on the Australian goldfields with a specific meaning, 'the waste from a mine', and is now current both in this context and, less widely, in a more general sense.

Nugget is the only word in this group to have set the etymologists off. A dialect word for 'a lump of anything' recorded in Ireland, Scotland and parts of England (notably Cornwall), *nugget* came into use in Australia in the fifties in two distinct senses:

> The word nugget among farmers signifies a small compact beast—a runt; among gold miners a lump, in contradistinction to the scale or dust gold.[73]

The two meanings of the adjective *nuggety* maintain this distinction, but the verb *to nugget* means either 'to pick out nuggets',[74] or 'to appropriate an unbranded calf'. In 1852, only shortly after it came into general use in Australia, *nugget* attracted the attention of the etymologists and an interesting correspondence ensued in *Notes and Queries*, one writer suggesting a Persian derivation, another describing *nugget* as an American corruption of *ingot*, and a third producing a list of related dialectal forms which clinched the word's derivation and meaning.[75]

The character and extent of these survivals demonstrate the importance of the contribution made by regional dialect vocabularies to Australian English. Some words which had a limited currency in their place of origin have achieved a general currency here and a few have gone even further, becoming established in the standard vocabulary of British English as well as that of Australian. The provenance of these words can often not be established with any great precision: they were clearly in use

[73] Mundy, *Our Antipodes*, vol. 3, p. 322.

[74] R. Cecil, *Gold Fields Diary*, p. 31.

[75] *Notes and Queries*, ser. 1, vol. 6 (1852), pp. 171, 281; vol. 7 (1853), pp. 144, 272, 366, 393; vol. 8 (1854), p. 481.

in one or more of the regional dialect areas, most commonly in those adjacent to the growing urban concentrations. But in only one instance, the survival of a handful of Cornish mining terms, is there clear evidence of the survival of a number of related terms from a single dialect area.

The character of the words is exactly that which the historical evidence would lead us to expect: the number of words relating specifically to rural occupations is small, most of the survivals being as much at home in the colloquial speech of the cities as in that of the country. Some even come into Australian English through the medium of city slang, further evidence of a general fluidity in the vulgar colloquial vocabulary of the early nineteenth century.

Many are now unfamiliar, if not obsolete, though their use in nineteenth-century Australian English can be demonstrated from written sources. How representative a selection these make it is impossible to tell. There may have been many more words in use in colloquial speech—either in particular areas or amongst particular classes of people—and the full extent of the survival of dialect words in Australian English is something at which, until a contemporary dialect survey is made, one can only guess. There are, for instance, a number of familiar words, like *smarmy* and *smoodge*, which are known to most Australians but whose histories are hard to document, and the sudden emergence in colloquial speech of a word like *scungy*, meaning 'clinging, fawning' and hence 'unpleasant' and often 'dirty', suggests, again, a body of dialect survivals with a long, but unrecorded, history in Australian speech.

5

The Language of the Settlers: Innovations

As the First Fleet left the Cape of Good Hope David Collins wrote in his journal:

> It was natural for the thinking part of the colonists to indulge at this moment a melancholy reflection which obtruded itself upon the mind. The land behind them was the abode of a civilised people; that before them was the residence of savages: when, if ever, they might again enjoy the commerce of the world, was very uncertain. The refreshments and pleasures of which they had so liberally partaken at the Cape, were to be exchanged for coarse fare and hard labour at New South Wales. All communication with families and friends now cut off, they were leaving the world behind them, to enter on a state unknown.[1]

New, strange, and barbarous it certainly seemed to them on their arrival. Struck either with the excitement of discovery or with the despair of exiles they surveyed the new land, its animal life, its 'numerous, curious, and beautiful birds', and its 'not less various and curious' vegetable productions; and many 'ingenious gentlemen', as Paterson noted, 'while discharging the most arduous and important offices, . . . snatched an hour to communicate to their friends in Europe some uncommon production of this vast country'.[2] Paterson himself, introducing a chapter on the natural history of the settlement, wrote:

> The woods and fields present a boundless variety of the choicest productions of nature, which gratify the senses with their fragrance and magnificence; while the

[1] *An Account of the English Colony in New South Wales* (1910 ed.), p. 9.
[2] *The History of New South Wales*, p. 417.

branches of the trees display a brilliant assemblage of the feathered race, whose plumage, 'glittering in the sun', dazzles the eye of the beholder with its unmatched loveliness and lustre, and presenting, on the whole, a scene too rich for the pencil to pourtray—too glowing and animated for the feeble pen of mortal to describe with half the energy and beauty which belong to it, and without which description is unfaithful.[3]

Others, if they lacked Paterson's enthusiasm, shared his wonder at the variety of what they saw, and, as they came to explore this strange and inhospitable land, the settlers found the need for words to label and describe what they saw both enormous and urgent. They encountered immediately trees, plants, birds, and animals which were new to them; they found the physical features of the new environment markedly different from the neat and ordered countryside they had left; and they observed tribes of native people who spoke in unfamiliar languages and whose food, dwellings, implements, weapons, and tribal customs were unlike anything they had seen before.

Just how quickly and how deliberately they went to work, and amongst which sections of the population the greater part of the expansion took place are questions which are not easy to answer. Morris remarks that,

unfortunately, names were not given by the best educated in the community, but often by those least qualified to invent satisfactory names: not by a linguist, a botanist, an ornithologist, an ichthyologist, but by the ordinary settler.[4]

By and large he is right. There are a few instances, in the naming of flora and fauna particularly, when well-qualified people, or people who were at least, for various reasons, careful of the language, chose names. The explorer, T. L. Mitchell, for instance, assiduously collected the Aboriginal names of places, flora, and fauna, and a few of these, words like *goborro*, *quandong*, and *yarrah*, later came into general use (see p. 34 above). *Bettong*, *boobook*, and

[3] Ibid., p. 416.
[4] *Austral English*, p. xii.

budgerigar, similarly, were Aboriginal names collected and recorded by the first investigators to sight and describe these creatures. And there are a few names of plants which commemorate botanical observers, *banksia*, for instance, named after Sir Joseph Banks and in use in Australia by 1790,[5] and *boronia*, named after Francesco Borone, a friend of the botanist, J. E. Smith. But these make up a small and generally atypical part of the vocabulary. Usually we can do no more than attribute words, as Morris did, to 'the man in the bush'; and it is through an analysis of the ways in which this anonymous immigrant found words to express himself that the essential characteristics of the Australian vocabulary can be distinguished.

What the earliest visitors to New South Wales notice first are the Aboriginal words (see chapter 6) and those current in British English which have been given a more generalized or at least slightly altered meaning in their new environment. As early as 1805, for instance, Governor King distinguishes between the Australian use of *brush*, which he defines as 'a dark, impenetrable thicket consisting of plants and herbacious Shrubs'; *scrub*, which he classifies as 'a local expression' and defines as 'consisting of Shrubs of low growth, Soil of a bad quality with small Iron gravelly Stones'; and *forest land*, which

> is such as abounds with Grass and is the only Ground which is fit to Graze; according to the local distinction [he adds] the Grass is the discriminating Character and not the Trees, for by making use of the Former it is clearly understood as different from a Brush or Scrub.[6]

Although not all the distinctions that King made have been retained, they are clear and obviously important to him if he was to give any sort of accurate account of the terrain he was describing; and each word had for him a meaning different from that it would have had for his Colonial Office correspondent. *Brush*, in British English, meant 'a thicket of small trees or underwood'; in Aus-

---

[5] See T. Watling, *Letters from an exile at Botany Bay*, p. 16, and J. White, *Journal of a Voyage to New South Wales*, p. 221.

[6] *H.R.A.*, vol. v, p. 586.

tralian English, because it was used of the sub-tropical vegetation of the New South Wales coastal regions, *brush*'s meaning was extended to include 'a dense growth of forest as well as of undergrowth'. The meaning of *forest* was likewise adapted so that it could be used not only of densely wooded country but of the open, sparsely timbered country of New South Wales; and *scrub*, from meaning 'low growth, brushwood', or a tract of country overgrown with this, was extended to take account also of country overgrown with thick, and often heavy, bush.

Other words for physical features underwent a similar change or extension of meaning. In the same passage King records *creek* and *lagoon*, both as 'local expressions'. *Creek*, he says, is 'applied to all brooks and small Rills that are deeply seated in the Ground and the Sides or Banks very Steep'.[7] This is the same meaning as had developed in American English in the seventeenth century but, almost certainly, the Australian use was an independent result of exactly the same process of extension. In British English the use of *creek* at the time was restricted to an estuary or arm of the sea, and the *Oxford English Dictionary*'s note on the American and colonial use of the word shows clearly what had happened: it describes *creek* as the name probably given originally by the explorers of a river to the various inlets or arms observed to run from it, of which only the mouths were seen in passing. When at a later period these (so-called) *creeks* were explored they were often found to be tributaries of greater length, but retained nonetheless the designation they had originally been given. *Lagoon* underwent a less dramatic change: used in British English of ponds of salt or brackish water separated from the sea by low sandbanks, it was extended very early in Australian usage to refer also to ponds of fresh water, usually but not invariably stagnant, formed by a creek or spring.

A second and more extensive group of words whose meanings were extended is that made up of names of trees

7 Ibid.

found by the colonists. Many of these were descriptive compounds (see p. 86 below), but a good number were named because of the supposed resemblance of their foliage, wood, or fruit to that of a familiar English tree, something which Mundy noticed in 1852:

> Most of the Trees, or rather of the timbers, of this colony owe their names to the sawyers who first tested their qualities. They were guided by the colour and character of the wood, knowing and caring nothing about botanical relations. Thus the swamp-oak and the she-oak have rather the exterior of the larch than any quercine aspect. Pomona would indignantly disown the apple-tree, for there is not the semblance of a pippin on its tufted branches. A shingle of the beef-wood resembles a cypress, but is of a tenderer green, bearing a worthless little berry, having its stone or seed outside . . . the pear-tree is, I believe, an eucalypt, and bears a pear of solid wood, hard as heart of oak. . . .[8]

This dismay is fairly frequently voiced. James Back-house's description of the *cherry-tree*, for instance, rings with exasperation:

> . . . the Cherry-Tree is an Exocarpus—a leafless, green, cypress-like bush, with small red and white fruit, bearing the stone outside.[9]

But there were others who felt that the similarities were obvious. Dawson, in 1831, wrote that:

> The resemblance of what are called apple-trees in Australia, to those of the same name at home, is so striking at a distance in these situations, that the comparisons could not be avoided, although the former bear no fruit, and do not even belong to the same species.[10]

In some cases the resemblance to an English species was sufficient for the choice of name, but a qualification was introduced through the use of a particularizer, as, for

---

[8] *Our Antipodes*, vol. II, pp. 25-6.
[9] *Narrative of a Visit to the Australian Colonies*, p. 22.
[10] *The Present State of Australia*, p. 195.

instance, in *Huon pine, Moreton Bay chestnut, Moreton Bay fig, native indigo,* and *native pear.*[11]

What is surprising is the rapidity with which some of these names became generally current, occurring in surveyors' reports to the Governor, and in the Governor's reports to the Colonial Office—in passages of formal English, in other words, which we would normally expect to be conservative. So *apple-tree, box, cherry-tree, mahogany, native pear,* and *oak* were in use before 1810, *cedar, honeysuckle, Huon pine,* and *Moreton Bay chestnut* before 1840.

In all these cases, where the words are names for geographical features or for trees, the extension of meaning is easily explained: a word in fairly general use in England was used in Australia because the resemblances, in appearance or utility, were felt to be stronger than the differences and, perhaps, at such a distance from England, because the differences seemed of little account.

There are many other words, from different contexts, by which the same process could be illustrated. Words like *paddock* and *run,* for instance, are used here to denote larger areas than they were in England. *Mob,* which in England was used either of a disorderly rabble or of the lower classes generally (in both senses with disparaging implications), was in use in Australia, with reference to stock, before 1840.

Gutter, reef, and *shepherd* were given new applications on the Australian goldfields, *gutter* acquiring a technical meaning, 'the lower part of the channel of an old river of the Tertiary period, containing auriferous deposits',[12] and *reef* similarly being used of a lode or vein of auriferous quartz or of the bedrock. *Shepherd,* perhaps because of the general contempt for shepherds who worked on sheep stations, in contrast to stockmen, came to mean 'to hold

---

[11] One example of this, now completely disguised, is *rosella,* a corruption of *rosehiller,* which is itself an abbreviation for *rosehill parrot,* the name given to a parrot found near the Governor's residence, 'Rosehill' at Parramatta.

[12] *Oxford English Dictionary.*

possession of a claim by doing the minimum amount of work required by the mining by-laws'.

The same process, at a somewhat different level, is evident in the histories of *bludger* and *cove*. *Bludger* is recorded in Hotten's *Dictionary of Modern Slang, Cant and Vulgar Words* (compiled in England in the mid-nineteenth century), with the meaning 'a low thief, who does not hesitate to use violence'. By the end of the century it is in use in Australia, its meaning somewhat more specific, 'a thief who will use his bludgeon and lives on the gains of immoral women'.[13] There has been a gradual weakening of this sense in contemporary usage and, although something of the word's early connotations remain, it is now used widely of a person who evades his responsibilities and imposes on others. *Cove* also comes from English slang. Vaux notes that 'the master of a house or shop is sometimes called a cove', and its later meaning of 'station-manager' presumably developed from this.

In a few instances there is a metaphoric usage behind the extension of meaning. This is possibly what happened with *cockatoo* (whence the now more commonly used *cocky*), which may, as A. G. Mitchell suggests, refer to the small farmer's 'habit of alighting on land to extract good from it';[14] it certainly explains *currency*, which came into general use before 1830 in the contrasting of *currency*, 'native-born', and *sterling*, 'immigrant'. Other examples are the use of *to prop*, originally of a horse 'propping dead on his forelegs', and *rosella*, the name of a scarlet-breasted parrot applied to a sheep which has lost a portion of its wool. Occasionally words have changed their meaning by a process of association: *selection* (or *free selection*), the choosing of a piece of land under the Land laws came, by the end of the century, to be a synonym for the land itself; *wattle*, an English word used (either as a noun or verb) of branches and twigs twined together to make fences and

13 Crowe, *Australian Slang Dictionary*.
14 *Supplement of Australian and New Zealand Words*, in *Chambers's Shorter English Dictionary*.

walls, came, before 1830, to be used of the tree found most suitable for this purpose in Australia.

There is one group of closely related words which illustrates the way in which words extend their meaning particularly well. These are *hut, hutkeeper, muster, overseer, station,* and *superintendent.* All were first used in Australian English, with their established meanings, as part of the vocabulary describing convict settlements and their routines; but all have subsequently shifted slightly in meaning to take in the not dissimilar set of referents on sheep and cattle runs.

Hut and *hutkeeper* have moved together, the one referring to the convicts' living quarters, the other to the person, usually a woman or an old man, who kept the hut clean and provided food for the men on their return. In a passage written in 1794, in *Slavery and Famine,* G. Thompson describes the hutkeeper's functions and prospects:

> At night they [the convicts] are placed in a hut, perhaps 14, 16 or 18 together (with one woman, whose duty is to keep it clean, and provide victuals for the men while at work) . . . The women have a more comfortable life than the men; those who are not fortunate enough to be selected for wives . . . are made hut keepers.[15]

In 1831 *hutkeeper* was used of an Aboriginal who looked after the hut of an emancipist,[16] and by 1840 it meant the man or woman who kept a stockman's hut clean, fed the man or men who lived in the hut, and sometimes watched the sheep at night. A verb, *to hutkeep,* is found with this meaning in the 1840s.

Muster was the word regularly used by the Governors of the colony when orders were issued for the assembly and inspecting of convicts. It is a word out of a military context and would naturally have been used by the military in the colony with reference to any assembly. But as early as 1813 both noun and verb were in use in the colony with reference to cattle rather than convicts.[17] And so fully is this

15 *Slavery and Famine, Punishment for Sedition,* pp. 36-7.
16 Dawson, *The Present State of Australia,* p. 88.
17 *H.R.A.,* vol. vii, pp. 741, 745.

meaning established in Australia that we tend to think of it as the primary meaning, and of loosely used expressions like *a full muster*, or *not a bad muster* as being derived from the word as it is used in the handling of stock. *Overseer* and *superintendent* followed similar courses. Both were used of officers in charge of convict gangs or stations and were subsequently used, *overseer* by 1822 and *superintendent* by 1836,[18] of the manager of a farm or station. The shortened form of *superintendent, super,* is recorded by the *Oxford English Dictionary* in 1870, but was almost certainly in use earlier and is still current.

The word out of this group that is most widely current now is *station*. In Australian English *station* meant firstly a government outpost or a place at which convicts were employed or housed. This was a natural development of the word's use with reference to any sort of outpost and it is not surprising to find it used also, in the early period, of missionary establishments. One sort of outpost was that at which herds of government stock were grazed inland from the settlement at Port Jackson, and *station* is first recorded in this sense in 1815:

> The land lying between Mount Hunter, the creek, and the river . . . being well calculated for that purpose, it is my intention to form an establishment here for at least three separate herds of the Government horned cattle, at three distinct stations.[19]

Settlers who owned sheep or cattle followed the government practice, so by the 1820s *station* was being used of any tract of land on which sheep or cattle were grazed under the supervision of an *overseer*. As the word came into general currency many compounds were formed, among them *back station, cattle station, head station, out-station, sheep station, station-hand, station-house, station owner,* and *stock station*.

This sort of gradual extension of a word's meaning, its

18 Ibid., vol. x, p. 788 and vol. xviii, p. 797.
19 *Lachlan Macquarie, Governor of New South Wales: Journals of his Tours in New South Wales and Van Diemen's Land, 1810-22,* p. 120.

adaptation to new circumstances, is something which is occurring constantly in all languages; but it seems that these changes in early Australian English resulted to some extent at least from the depleted nature of the English the settlers brought to the colony, from the reduction in the number of words for features of the landscape and for pastoral and agricultural activities. Probably a more important way of expanding vocabulary and certainly a more productive one was the formation of compounds and full-word combinations. These, in Australian English, are almost always self-explanatory: straightforward and descriptive compounds formed from common English elements, like *blackbutt, bluegum, bottlebrush,* and *boundary rider.*

Many of the names for trees and plants have been formed in this way, one element being the name of the genus or supposed genus and one a particularizer of some sort, describing or identifying the species, as in the following: *apple gum, large-flowered swamp gum, pink gum, ghost gum* and *scribbly gum.* Far more of the trees and plants the settlers encountered have been named in this way than have been given Aboriginal names, yet this again should not be thought of as unique or taken as evidence of the inventiveness of the Australian. In Marckwardt's *American English* there is an analysis of the words used in the journals of an early scientific expedition travelling across the continent: of over 700 terms recorded, more than one-third are compounds.[20] The character of Australian compounds and full-word combinations can perhaps best be illustrated if the full list is broken into groups.

1 FLORA

beefwood	cutting grass
blackboy	flooded gum
blackbutt	grass tree
bluegum	he-oak
bottlebrush	ironbark
celery-topped pine	kangaroo apple

[20] *American English,* p. 87.

kangaroo grass	raspberry-jam wood
lightwood	saltbush
native cucumber	she-oak
native indigo	stringybark
native orange tree	swamp oak
native pear	tea tree

Almost all of these, it is obvious at first glance, are descriptive, either of the appearance of the tree or of some quality of its wood. *Beefwood* was so called for the redness of its wood, *ironbark*, *lightwood*, and *stringybark* for the qualities of the timber which the name indicates. The exotically named *raspberry-jam wood* was so called because 'it emits, when cut, an odour precisely similar to that of raspberry jam'.[21] Others were so named for their appearance: *blackbutt*, *bluegum*, and *bottlebrush* explain themselves; the *blackboy* was so called because, from its appearance in the distance, it may fancifully be compared to an Aboriginal, the *celery-topped pine* because of 'the resemblance of a branch clothed with its dilated leaves, to the leaf of Celery'.[22] The *flooded gum* and *swamp oak* were so called after their natural habitat, the *tea tree* because a substitute for tea was made by settlers and bushrangers from its leaves, and the *saltbush* because of its alkaline character.

Many of these, like the extensions in meaning of existing English tree-names, were in use very early: Thompson, in 1794, distinguished the *he-oak* from the *she-oak*,[23] and, in 1801, Surveyor Grimes, reporting on a tour of the Hunter River district, noted the occurrence of *blackbutt*, *bluegum*, *ironbark* and *stringybark*.[24] *Swamp oak* and *tea tree* were also in use by then;[25] with the exception of *bottlebrush*, all the words in this list were in use before 1860.

[21] J. Capper, *Our Gold Colonies*, p. 9.
[22] J. Backhouse, *Narrative of a Visit to the Australian Colonies*, p. 48.
[23] *Slavery and Famine*.
[24] *H.R.A.*, vol. III, p. 414.
[25] Ibid., p. 170.

2   FAUNA

bronzewing	lyrebird
bulldog ant	morepork
bushman's clock	native companion
coachman	native dog
emu-wren	native turkey
forester kangaroo	razor grinder
kangaroo dog	redbill
kangaroo-rat	swamp pheasant
laughing jackass	whipbird

All of these names, like those in the preceding section, were in use before 1860, some of them very early. *Kangaroo-rat*, for instance, the name of a small marsupial called by the Aborigines *potoroo*, was used by Governor Phillip in 1788.[26] The animal had something of the novelty of the kangaroo and an obvious similarity in appearance, and the descriptive compound quickly ousted the Aboriginal *potoroo*. *Bettong*, the Aboriginal name for another genus of kangaroo-rat, has similarly dropped out of use (see p. 118 below).

Several of these compounds describe either the physical appearance of the animal or one of its more striking characteristics, and one or two of them took some time to settle into their present form, having to compete with different forms or with rival and similarly descriptive words. *Bronzewing*, for instance, was first described as the *golden-winged pigeon*,[27] later as the *bronze-winged pigeon*, a name which was shortened by the 1850s to *bronzewing*.

Similarly, the *whipbird*, which is first recorded in 1822 in its fullest form, *coachman's whipbird*,[28] is shortened to *coachman* and to *whipbird*, the latter form becoming current in the 1840s.[29] Cunningham, in 1827, gives a pleasant illustration of the context which gave rise to the name:

---

[26] *Historical Records of New South Wales (H.R.N.S.W.)*, vol. I, pt ii, p. 135.

[27] White, *Voyage to New South Wales*, p. 145.

[28] B. Field, *Journal of an Excursion across the Blue Mountains*, p. 42.

[29] See J. Cotton, *Correspondence 1842-1849*, p. 10.

You meet with some adventures probably both to astonish and alarm you, but these mostly end in your amusement. If you should hear a coach-whip crack behind, you may instinctively start aside to let *the mail* pass, but quickly find it is only our native *coachman* with his spread-out fan-tail and perked-up crest, whistling and cracking out his whiplike notes as he hops sprucely from branch to branch.[30]

An even more distinctive sound, the laugh of the kookaburra, was variously described in several imaginative compounds. The earliest and, throughout the nineteenth century, the most common of these is *laughing jackass*, a name used first by Collins in 1798 in a vocabulary of Aboriginal words (the word it explains being *gi-gan-ne-gine*, like *kookaburra* itself onomatopoeic).[31] Cunningham's comment on *laughing jackass* is again useful as it pinpoints the reason behind three of the early alternative popular names, *bushman's clock*, *Hawkesbury clock*, and *settler's clock*:

> Nor are we without our rural noters of the time to call us to our early task, and warn us of evening's close. The loud and discordant noise of the *laughing jackass* (or *settler's clock*, as he is called), as he takes up his roost on the withered bough of one of our tallest trees, acquaints us that the sun has just dipped behind the hills, and that it is time to trudge homewards.[32]

Two other birds whose names derive from their calls are the *morepork*, where the name is imitative of the sound (see p. 122 below), and *razor grinder*, the Australian Dishwasher or Restless Flycatcher, where the name is descriptive of the sound. Other names, like *redbill* and *lyrebird*, describe a bird's most distinctive physical characteristic, and the same is true of names, like *native dog* (for 'dingo') and *native turkey*, in which, by the addition of a particularizing adjective, an analogy is drawn between the Australian and the familiar English species. The naming of the *emu-wren* illustrates both these processes:

[30] *Two Years in New South Wales* (2nd ed.), vol. II, p. 150.
[31] *Account of the English Colony in New South Wales*, p. 615.
[32] *Two Years in New South Wales* (2nd ed.), vol. I, p. 217.

The decomposed or loose structure of these [tail] feathers, much resembling those of the Emu, has suggested the colonial name of Emu Wren for this species, an appellation singularly appropriate, inasmuch as it at once indicates the kind of plumage with which the bird is clothed, and the wren-like nature of its habits.[33]

In other instances names were given because of the characteristic behaviour of the animal: the *native companion*, a large crane, was probably so called because it was most commonly found in flocks,[34] the *forester kangaroo* and the *swamp pheasant* because of the type of country in which they were found, the *kangaroo dog* after the purpose for which it was bred, and the *bulldog ant* after the ferocity of a bite which early impressed itself on travellers.

3   PASTORAL ACTIVITIES

backblocks	station-house
back run	station owner
back station	stockbook
boundary rider	stock-farm
cattle run	stock-holder
cattle station	stockhorse
gullyrake	stock-house
head station	stock-hut
outback	stock-keeper
out-sheep station	stockman
out-squatter	stock-route
out-station	stock run
sheep run	stock station
sheep station	stockwhip
sliprail	stockyard
station-hand	woolshed

The most noticeable feature of this list of words, and the most interesting in that it demonstrates how the everyday vocabulary of the settlers was extended to meet their needs, is the number of compounds or full-word combinations which are built on one of the commonly

[33] J. Gould, *Birds of Australia*, vol. III, plate 31.
[34] See *brolga* (p. 122 below); the earliest use of *native companion* I have found is in B. Field, *Journal of an Excursion* (1822), p. 45.

used words like *run, station,* or *stock.* The earliest compound with *stock* as its key element is *stockyard,* in use before 1800[35] and apparently used initially in a wider sense than it is today. Governor King refers in 1803 to the enclosure of 'great extents of Ground', and Macquarie, in 1813, talks of having

> an equal Number of good Substantial Strong Stock Yards erected in proper and Suitable parts of the Country, where it is intended the Government Cattle shall in future Graze, for the purpose of Collecting and lodging them in at Nights, as well as on Occasions of Mustering and Marking them.[36]

King's usage suggests, as the editor of this part of his correspondence in the *Historical Records of Australia* noted, not 'the limited sense of the present day' but 'a meaning similar to that expressed by the modern word paddock'.[37] *Yard* was used in the general sense of *enclosure* and it was only after the need for a particular sort of enclosure became apparent that the meaning of the word was narrowed.

The person who supervised these operations was, about 1800, called either a *stock-keeper* or a *stockman,* but the latter term seems, even then, to have been preferred. Here again the meaning of a word has narrowed. Originally *stockman* seems to have been used of one who tended cattle or sheep but, from as early as the 1820s, there is evidence of a distinction between 'stockmen and sheep watchmen'[38] or 'Shepherds and Stockmen'.[39] Later combinations, all of which were in use before 1830, include *stock-farm, stock-holder, stock-house, stock-hut, stock run,* and *stock station.*

The use of the particularizers, *back-, head-,* and *out-,* provides a further example of the way the colonists took,

[35] *H.R.A.,* vol. II, p. 21.
[36] Ibid., vol. IV, p. 310 and vol. VII, p. 745.
[37] Ibid., vol. VII, p. 741.
[38] Field, *Journal of an Excursion* (1822), p. 45.
[39] F. Tuckfield to the Secretary, Wesleyan Missionary Society, 1841.

and adapted, the first word to hand. The usage is explained in the following two quotations:

> At squatting stations there is generally what is called a home, or head-station, around which, according to the extent of stock, 'out-stations' are established.[40]

> An out-station is simply a hut built at a convenient distance from the homestead, or from any other Out-station on the 'run' or sheep-walk, so as to allow ample feeding-ground for two flocks of sheep.[41]

Out- had a more general application in British English, and words like *outsettler* and *outsettlement* are recorded from the eighteenth century. Both of these were in use in Australia shortly after 1800, and words like *out-squatter*, which had a fairly short life, and *out-station* were presumably modelled on them. The use of *back-*, as in *back-blocks*, *back station*, and, further out still, *outback*, seems to replace *out-*, in its more general application, in the latter part of the century.[42]

The remaining words are mostly self-explanatory. The *sliprail*, or 'primitive gate of Australia',[43] belongs to the post-and-rail fence era, the earliest recorded use being that of Cunningham, in 1827:

> The pond might open into each field by a slip-rail entrance, so that whenever a field was under pasture, the rails might be taken down to admit the cattle.[44]

Woolshed, also, dates from about this time; *boundary rider* not till towards the end of the century. The verb *to gullyrake*, from which a noun *gullyraker* was formed, was explained by Alexander Harris in 1847:

> . . . gully-raking . . . this practice derives its name from the circumstance of cattle straying away from their own

---

[40] J. C. Byrne, *Twelve Years' Wandering* (1848), p. 189.

[41] Banister and Mossman, *Australia Visited and Revisited*, p. 65.

[42] *Back run*, on the other hand is early, being used specifically of grazing land separated from water by a station and therefore only useful as part of that station (*H.R.A.*, vol. xvii, p. 112).

[43] Mundy, *Our Antipodes*, vol. 3, p. 72.

[44] *Two Years in New South Wales* (2nd ed.), vol. 2, pp. 170-1.

herds into the bush, and forming wild herds which chiefly congregate down in the wild grassy gullies of the mountains . . . the gully-rakers eventually driving them out and branding all the young ones, and any others they can manage, with their own brands.[45]

The word does not seem to have been widely used in this sense, though it was used subsequently, the noun as the name for a stockwhip, the verb to describe the use of this whip and also in a quite unrelated sense, prospecting for gold.

4 BUSH LIFE

bush breakfast	bush life
bush costume	bushman
bush dinner	bush-ride
bushfire	bush road
bush horse	bush telegraph
bush house	cabbage tree hat
bush hut	colonial experience
bush language	kangaroo steamer
bush law	kangaroo-tail soup
bush-lawyer	leatherjacket

Only a selection of the nineteenth-century combinations which include *bush-* as their key element are listed here. Very many more could be added. Some, like *bushfire, bush horse, bush hut, bush life, bushman,* and *bush road,* all of which were in use before 1850, have settled into a more or less permanent form and meaning. *Bush-lawyer,* for 'one who fancies himself as being versed in the law', and *bush telegraph,* originally used of those who supplied bushrangers with information and later, more generally, of any 'grapevine' or 'rumour which passes along the grapevine', are both late nineteenth-century words which, in colloquial speech anyway, are equally settled. But most of the others seem to have been only casually compounded and have the character almost of nonce words. Examples of this are combinations like *bush breakfast* (of 'mutton,

---

[45] *Settlers and Convicts,* pp. 144-5.

damper and tea');[46] *bush costume* (of 'blue shirt, belt, and cabbage tree hat');[47] *bush dinner* (of 'mutton, damper, and tea'[48] again); *bush education*; *bush language* ('which may be better imagined than described');[49] *bush law*; and *bush-ride*.

During the late forties, and particularly during the fifties and sixties, words such as these were often used facetiously, both by Australians who were members of the bush fraternity and by itinerant Englishmen who were not; and the spurious currency they were given in journals of tours through the colony and, particularly, tours through the goldfields, has led to their importance being overstressed. They were never really part of the Australian vocabulary, and their use reflects the tendency of colloquial speech to use fashionable words, and the tendency of writers describing a society to adopt what is at first sight the most 'authentic' part of its vocabulary.

The other words in this group provide, again, an illustration of the simplest sort of word formation. *Cabbage tree hat*, for all the associations it now has with the legend of the bush, is a straight, descriptive compound, as is the probably obsolete *kangaroo steamer*, 'a very good colonial dish'[50] 'composed of steaks and chopped tail (with a few slices of salt pork), stewed with a very small quantity of water for a couple of hours in a close vessel'.[51] Of the two other foods named, *kangaroo-tail soup* was 'extolled as the most nourishing thing in nature' by one writer,[52] and the *leatherjacket*, 'a thin cake made of dough and put into a pan to bake with some fat', remarked on by another for the accuracy of its name: 'for tougher things cannot

---

[46] Byrne, *Twelve Years' Wandering*, p. 170.

[47] Banister and Mossman, *Australia Visited and Revisited*, p. 248.

[48] Capper, *Our Gold Colonies*, p. 33.

[49] Read, *What I Heard, Saw, and Did at the Australian Gold Fields*, p. 124.

[50] *New South Wales, Its Past, Present and Future Condition*, p. 73.

[51] Cunningham, *Two Years in New South Wales* (2nd ed.), vol. 1, p. 289. The earlier form, as used by Cunningham, is *steamer*.

[52] C. Rowcroft, *The Bushranger of Van Diemen's Land*, vol. 2, p. 285.

well be eaten'.[53] What it all added up to was *colonial experience,* an extraordinary expression which was used, both as a noun and an adjective, from the fifties on, to describe what all 'new chums' lacked.

5 ABORIGINES

blackfellow
blacktracker
breakweather
breakwind
walkabout

Two of these words, *blackfellow* and *walkabout* (see p. 111 below), have their origins in the Aboriginal pidgin of the twenties. The remaining three are later, *blacktracker,* used to describe an Aboriginal tracker employed by the police, coming into use in the sixties. *Breakweather* and *breakwind* make an interesting pair. Both were in use fairly early, *breakweather* by 1840[54] and *breakwind* by 1833[55] and both were first used in descriptions of the rough shelters erected by Aborigines. Thus Mundy, in *Our Antipodes,* describes

a large party of natives . . . camped behind the station, that is, squatted before a fire and behind a sloping sheet of bark turned from the wind—in bush lingo, a break-weather.[56]

Both words have the same meaning, the difference between the two being that one is formed from Standard English elements while the other, *breakweather,* is formed from Standard English *break* and dialect *weather,* meaning 'adverse or unpleasant weather'. Both were in use concurrently in the forties and fifties and it is probable that *breakweather* later dropped out of currency in face of the more generally used *breakwind.*

[53] Banister and Mossman, *Australia Visited and Revisited,* p. 126.
[54] A. Russell, *A Tour Through the Australian Colonies in 1839,* p. 84.
[55] J. Backhouse, Report on the State of the Settlement of the Van Diemen's Land Company, 1833, p. 6.
[56] Vol. 1, p. 331.

Other areas of the vocabulary expanded in this way
also: *goldfield*, now generally used in English, is probably
Australian in origin and, in the earliest years of the
colony, a number of new words were formed to describe
the workings of the convict system. *Government man*, for
instance, was one of the more commonly used euphemisms
for *convict*; *assigned servant* and *ticket-of-leaver* are examples of established English words which, in Australia,
acquired a fixed form and a set of special connotations.

In terms of numbers the formation of compounds is the
most important way in which the vocabulary of Australian
English has been expanded. Less significant are two other
sorts of change which also affect a word's form: a change
in its function, as in the formation of a verb, *to bush*,
from the noun, *bush*, and a change made in function and
form by the addition of a suffix, as in the formation of
First Fleeter from *First Fleet*. *To bush* was used in the
period before 1850 more or less in the sense of 'to rough
it':

> the style of country and of living, in this distant region,
> having no particular attraction, and not being provided
> for *bushing* it, in these early frosts, we made up our
> minds to return.[57]

This usage appears to have become obsolete in the latter
half of the century and is unrelated to the use of the past
participle, *bushed*, meaning 'lost', which was current then
in both literal and figurative usages. The colloquial noun
bushy, used with both favourable and unfavourable connotations for someone who is 'bush' born and bred, is
derived separately from the noun. A much earlier example
of this process is *emancipist*, a word used either as a noun
or an adjective of convicts who had served out their
sentences and formed during the 1820s from the verb *to
emancipate*.

Several new words were formed by the addition of an
-er suffix to existing words. Thus *bank* gave rise to *banker*,
commonly used of flooded rivers in the expressions 'to run
a banker' or 'to run half a banker'; *brickfield* to *brick-*

[57] W. J. Dumaresq, *A Ride to Bathurst* (1827), p. 99.

fielder, a now obsolete name used from the thirties in Sydney to describe a 'southerly buster' (*Brickfield* survives in the place-name Brickfield Hill in Sydney); *First Fleet* to *First Fleeter*, which had acquired a respectable status as early as 1830;[58] *offside* to *offsider*, used at the end of the century of the 'offside' (as opposed to 'near-side') bullocks in a team, and now generally current in colloquial speech in the sense of 'assistant, mate'; and *to overland* (itself Australian, formed from an existing English adjective) to *overlander*, used from the forties of one who drove stock for long distances cross-country.

These are casual formations. There are others, much rarer, which are more deliberate, whose coiners were conscious of the fact that they were coining new words to meet specific needs. James Mudie, for instance, coined *felonry*, and used it in the title of his book, after which it has moved into more general currency. 'The author', he wrote,

has ventured to coin the word *felonry*, as the appellative of an *order* or class of persons in New South Wales,— an order which happily exists in no other country in the world. The major part of the inhabitants of the colony are felons now undergoing or felons who have already undergone their sentences. They occupy not only the station of the peasantry and labourers in other civilized communities, but many—very many—of them are also, as respects their wealth or their pursuits, in the condition of gentry, or of dealers, manufacturers, merch-ants, and lawyers or other members of the liberal professions. Hitherto there was no single term that could be employed to designate these various descrip-tions of persons, who now bear the denominations of 'convicts' and 'ticket-of-leave-men'; as also, 'emancipists', (as they are absurdly enough called), who again are subdivided into 'conditionally pardoned convicts', 'fully pardoned convicts', and 'expirees', or transported felons whose sentences have expired; together with 'runaway convicts', subdivided into 'absentees', (a name foolish for its mildness), and 'bushrangers'. The single term, the *felonry* (which comprehends all these descriptions

58 *H.R.A.*, vol. xv, p. 371.

of the criminal population), though new, is evidently a legitimate member of the tribe of appellatives distinguished by the same termination, as *peasantry, tenantry, yeomanry, gentry, cavalry, chivalry, etc.* The author has the honour of especially presenting it to the *gentlemen* emancip*ists, alias,* the emancip*ated* felons of the colony, by whom he has no doubt it will be received with most peculiar approbation and delight, inasmuch as it not only expresses—and elegantly expresses—their place in society, but as it raises their *caste* (with all the beauty and fashion of the *felonry* of New South Wales, whether sparkling in silks and jewels at the theatre and the ball, or dashing four-in-hand to the races at Parramatta, or over the glittering and crowded 'drive' to Bellevue Point, on the South Head Road, not more romantic by the magnificence of its natural scenery than by the living splendours of its rich and animated *felonry*), to the dignity of an *order* in the commonwealth.[59]

This is a quite remarkable instance of coinage in that the writer both declares his intention of inventing the word and demonstrates the need for it in the thesis he later develops.

If the popular etymology is to be believed *jackeroo* is another example, though its historical development is not as well documented. A synonym for *colonial experiencer,* and for the New Zealand use of *cadet, jackeroo* is popularly supposed to be a corruption of *Johnny* or *Jacky Raw* formed in imitation of *kangaroo*. But derivations from an Aboriginal language and from one of the South American native languages have also been suggested.[60]

We can distinguish, then, three ways in which the Australian settlers, drawing on the resources of the vocabulary they had, met the demands of their new environment: the generalization or extension of the meanings of existing English words; the formation of descriptive compounds and full-word compositions; and the altering of the form and function of existing English words to give them new uses. Borrowings were made from the Aboriginal languages

59 J. Mudie, *The Felonry of New South Wales* (1837), p. xiii.
60 *Bulletin*, 4 October 1933, p. 20; 22 November 1933, p. 21.

and, from the beginning of the goldrush period, there was a further influx of words from the English regional dialects and from American English; but these remain, throughout the nineteenth century, the most significant means of expansion.

The parallels with the development of American English are always close, although the pattern of American English becomes increasingly more complex with borrowings from other immigrant European languages and the development within American English of a number of regional dialects. In both societies there was, of necessity, a considerable expansion of the existing vocabulary. In both this perhaps happened more freely because the societies were, in a sense, 'frontier' societies, without many of the restraints which had operated in British English. But in both the methods of expansion used were substantially the same; and to claim that, in either case, the resourcefulness and inventiveness shown in the creation of new words is unique, or 'a sign of a vigorous and developing national life',[61] is to be extravagantly chauvinistic and to ignore the fact that these methods of expansion were, and continue to be, the most common in all branches of English.[62]

[61] A view opposed by A. G. Mitchell in 'Australian English', *Australian Quarterly*, March 1951, p. 14.

[62] See Marckwardt, *American English*, pp. 81-109; R. C. Simonini, Jr., 'Etymological Categories of Present-Day English and their Productivity', *Language Learning*, vol. 9 (1959), no. 1, pp. 1-5.

6

Borrowings from Aboriginal Languages

BY AN ODD CHANCE the first Aboriginal word to be used in English was borrowed some eighteen years before the arrival of the First Fleet and 'introduced' to the Aborigines by the first settlers at Port Jackson. The word was *kangaroo* and the novelty of 'the leaping quadruped' sighted by Cook and his party at Endeavour River in 1770 was enough to bring *kangaroo* into immediate currency, Phillip, Hunter, Tench, and others recognizing the animal from its description and using the word without hesitation. The Aborigines were less sure. Tench recorded that they used *kangaroo* indiscriminately for all animals except dogs, and describes having seen 'a party of Indians, busily employed in looking at some sheep in an inclosure, and repeatedly crying out, Kangaroo, kangaroo!'[1] Later, when he was exhibiting to the Aboriginal Colbee the cows brought out in *Gorgon*, Colbee asked if these were kangaroos.[2]

Their ignorance is easily explained and, in fact, taught the colonists their first lesson about the Aboriginal languages. Whenever possible the members of Cook's expedition collected vocabularies of native words and Phillip, when he arrived at Port Jackson in 1788, was armed with a vocabulary of Aboriginal words collected at Endeavour River and hopeful that this would provide him with a means of conversing with the Port Jackson Aborigines. But, as he wrote to Banks, he quickly found that the

language was totally different not only from the language

[1] Tench, *Complete Account of the Settlement at Port Jackson*, p. 51.
[2] Ibid., p. 269.

of the Endeavour River natives but also from the languages spoken by Tribes in the immediate vicinity of Port Jackson, north of the Hawkesbury River for instance, and inland towards the Blue Mountains.[3]

The Endeavour River vocabulary with which the settlers arrived was thus of no practical use and is in fact of little interest except for its record of *kangaroo* and of one other word, *quoll*, and for the account which Banks gives of the rather chancy method of collection:

Of their Language I can say very little. Our acquaintance with them was of so short a duration that none of us attempted to use a single word of it to them, consequently the list of words I have given could be got no other manner than by signs enquiring of them what in their Language signified such a thing, a method obnoxious to many mistakes: for instance a man holds in his hand a stone and asks the name of [it]: the Indian may return him for answer either the real name of a stone, one of the properties of it as hardness, roughness, smoothness &c, one of its uses or the name peculiar to some particular species of stone, which name the enquirer immediately sets down as that of a stone. To avoid however as much as Possible this inconvenience Myself and 2 or 3 more got from them as many words as we could, and having noted down those which we though[t] from circumstances we were not mistaken in we compard our lists; those in which all the lists agreed, or rather were contradicted by none, we thought our selves moraly certain not to be mistaken in. Of these my list cheefly consists, some only being added that were in only one list such as from the ease with which signs might be contrivd to ask them were thought little less certain than the others.[4]

It is possible, as it turns out, that *kangaroo* did not mean to the Endeavour River Aborigines what it meant to Cook, that a misunderstanding of the sort foreseen by Banks did in fact occur. When Captain King visited Endeavour

---

[3] Phillip to Banks, 2 July 1788 (Banks Papers).
[4] J. C. Beaglehole, *The Endeavour Journal of Joseph Banks, 1768-1771*, vol. 2, p. 136.

River in 1827 he found that, although most of the words recorded by Cook's party were still current, the natives did not recognize *kangaroo*, using in its place a hitherto unrecorded word, *menuah*. This discovery led to the ingenious theory that *kangaroo*, uttered in response to an explorer's inquiry, meant nothing more than 'I do not know' or 'I do not understand'; but this is hardly probable and the most likely explanation of the word's 'disappearance' is that two different species of the animal had been confused.[5] Whatever had happened, by the time King's expedition raised doubts about the word's origin, *kangaroo* was firmly established in English and had even been used as the name of a ship, the brig *Kangaroo*, commissioned in 1814. *Quoll*, the name of a much less exciting animal, was less fortunate. It became part of the scientific name for a native cat, *Dasyurus quoll*, but achieved no wider currency.

Of much more interest and use in tracking down the origins of Aboriginal borrowings are the early vocabularies compiled in the Port Jackson area. The knowledge that there were many different Aboriginal languages in the colony and that the Port Jackson language was spoken, in Governor Phillip's estimate, by no more than 1,500 people, did nothing to inhibit borrowing. The words used by the local natives were readiest to hand and their vocabulary was an obvious first source of names for the flora and fauna of the colony, and for the implements and dwellings of the Aborigines themselves. We find, therefore, that the number of words in general use which derive from the Port Jackson language or from languages once spoken in the areas about Sydney is greater than that from any other part of the country. Almost one-tenth of the 250-odd words collected by Hunter in 1790 are still current in Australian English today, about five times as many as were borrowed from any other Aboriginal language. The same sort of phenomenon can be seen in the history of American English, where a substantial proportion of words of Indian origin still generally current were borrowed from one or other of the Algonquian languages,

[5] See T. Iredale and E. Troughton, 'Captain Cook's Kangaroo', *Australian Zoologist*, 1925, pp. 311-16.

'the first to be encountered by the white men as they settled on the Atlantic coast'.[6]

Unfortunately, the material for the historical study of these languages is far from adequate. Dictionaries range from those which are intended to provide as full a record as possible of the vocabularies of all accessible Aboriginal languages to those which aim at giving a list of words suitable for naming houses and beach cottages. But these are neither complete nor accurate, and none gives historical evidence for the derivation of words from particular dialects. The collections of the late nineteenth-century anthropologists are more useful. Curr, Mathew, and Roth preserve a number of the important early vocabularies, though the greater part of their material is drawn, like that of Smyth's, from untrained correspondents. Mathews, Ridley, and Taplin record vocabularies which they have in the main collected themselves from Aborigines.[7] But these are fairly late, the vocabularies of languages which were still extant at the time.

The great difficulty with these vocabularies, from the point of view of anyone interested in the effect of Aboriginal languages on Australian English, is that they are so late. They can be very useful for checking earlier lists but they do not provide a reliable means of pinning down the origin of Aboriginal words already in use in Australian English. As early as the 1830s Threlkeld north of Sydney and Lhotsky in the Monaro district had noticed the movement of words from one Aboriginal language to another, and the recording of *buckalow, bacala*, 'bullock', *picanini* and *tablety, tables*, 'travel', in Jorgen Jorgenson's vocabulary of a Tasmanian language in 1842 shows how English words have been adopted into Aboriginal languages and given forms which frequently conceal their origin. In

---

[6] Marckwardt, *American English*, p. 26.

[7] E. M. Curr, *The Australian Race*; J. Mathew, *Eaglehawk and Crow*; H. L. Roth, *The Aborigines of Tasmania*; R. B. Smyth, *The Aborigines of Victoria*; R. H. Mathews, Collected Articles on the Languages of the Australian Aborigines; W. Ridley, *Kamilaroi, Dippil and Turrubul* and *Kamilaroi and other Australian Languages*; G. Taplin, *The Narinyeri*.

H

addition to these sources of inaccuracy there is the strong possibility that an untrained recorder, hearing a word spoken, would transcribe it inaccurately, or Anglicize it, or, knowing an English or Aboriginal word for the referent already, suggest this to the speaker. Thus the word *waddy* is recorded in three early vocabularies as *wad-di* or *wad-dty*, *woo-da* and *woo-dah*, and its relation to English *wood* is uncertain.

In seeking to establish the derivation of what are apparently Aboriginal words, then, it is best to use these vocabularies as secondary evidence only and to rely where possible on vocabularies recorded by travellers and explorers in the first years of contact with the Aborigines. These again are far from complete and the languages which seem to have contributed most to Australian English are the least fully recorded: the vocabularies collected by C. G. Teichelmann and C. W. Schuermann around Adelaide and by Moore in Western Australia,[8] for instance, each within a few years of settlement, are longer and more comprehensive than those recorded by Hunter and Collins on the coast of New South Wales.

Four vocabularies of the language of the Port Jackson Aborigines survive: those compiled by Southwell in 1788, Hunter in 1790, Blackburn in 1791 and Collins in 1798.[9] None of these is the work of a trained observer, but the fullest, those of Hunter and Collins, have been compiled with care and together they provide evidence of the Port Jackson origin of a number of words which have since had some currency in Australian English: *baal* (a negative), *bogey*, 'to bathe', *boobook*, *budgeree*, *cobbra*, 'head', *cooee*, *corella*, *corroboree*, *currawong*, *dingo*, *gibber*, *gin*, *gunya*, *hielamon*, *jerran*, 'afraid', *kurrajong*, *mogo*, *murry* (an

[8] *Outline of a Grammar, Vocabulary, and Phraseology of the Aboriginal Language of South Australia*; G. F. Moore, *A Descriptive Vocabulary of the Language in Common Use amongst the Aborigines of Western Australia*.

[9] 'Journal and Letters of Daniel Southwell, 1788-1792' (Southwell Papers), *H.R.N.S.W.*, vol. II; J. Hunter, *Historical Journal of the Transactions at Port Jackson and Norfolk Island*, pp. 407-11; D. Blackburn, Papers; D. Collins, *Account of the English Colony in New South Wales*, vol. 1, pp. 610-15.

intensive), *myall, nulla nulla, pyalla,* 'to speak', *waddy, wallaby, warrigal, wollomai,* 'snapper', *woomera,* and *woomerang.* There is, of course, considerable variety in the spellings used, but spellings represent here not different pronunciations but different attempts at recording the Aboriginal pronunciation. Thus *boobook* is recorded as *pow-book* by Hunter and *bok-bok* by Blackburn; *kurrajong* as *cara-d'yung* by Southwell, *carra-'duin* by Hunter and *car-rah-jun* by Collins.

The early history of the English use of these words is often interesting. *Baal,* for instance, got away to a shaky start, as Tench records:

> The epithet wee-ree, signifying bad, we knew; and as the use of this word, and its opposite, afford the most simple form of denoting consent or disapprobation, to uninstructed Indians, in order to find out their word for good, when Arabanoo was first brought among us, we used jokingly to say, that anything, which he liked, was Weeree, in order to provoke him to tell us that it was good. When we said *Weeree,* he answered *Beeal,* which we translated, and adopted for good, whereas he meant no more than to simply deny our inference, and say, no —it is not bad.[10]

But, after this initial misunderstanding, the word quickly became established in Aboriginal pidgin and was widely used not only in New South Wales but through Queensland, the Northern Territory, and into Western Australia.

Bogey, or *bogie,* first recorded by Southwell in 1788 with the meaning of 'dive' but later used, both as a noun and verb, to mean 'bathe', and *budgeree,* meaning 'good', seem to have been widely current in the colloquial speech of the colony. Alexander Harris uses both words in *The Emigrant Family, budgeree* in passages of dialogue in which Aborigines are speaking. *Bogie* he describes as one of the most common words 'in daily parlance with all ranks'.[11]

Except, perhaps, in the north and west of Australia,

[10] *Complete Account,* p. 123.
[11] *Emigrant Family,* vol. 2, p. 175, vol. 1, p. 145.

budgeree has passed out of use, remaining only, as the result of a mistaken etymology, as the first part of *budgerigar*. This bird was first described by Gould, in his *Birds of Australia* (1848), and he gives it two names, *canary parrot*, the name used by the colonists, and *betcherrygah*, the name used by the Aborigines of the Liverpool Plains. In a later vocabulary of Kamilaroi, the language spoken in this district, *gijoriga* is given as the name of a small green parrot;[12] if we make allowance for the difficulty of recording in English the consonants used by the Aborigines, we can see that *betcherrygah* and *gijoriga* are probably different transcriptions of the same word. *Budgeree* is variously spelt: *boojery, boodgeree,* and *budgery* also occur and although there is no record of a pronunciation remotely like *betcherry*, it would seem that the wide currency of *budgeree*, and perhaps a hint of the meaning of 'good parrot' suggested by Morris, led to the new form, *budgerigar*, which is found during the 1850s.

Cobbra, the Port Jackson word for 'head' (which the *Oxford English Dictionary* erroneously derives from Malay) is used in an unlikely little song about a snake written in 1832:

> They with a stick effect would take
> Upon your cobra;
> While, round ye, little tadpoles make
> A great corrobra.[13]

And, although it seems never to have been as widely used as *bogie* or *budgeree,* it was sufficiently current in 1888 for Boldrewood to use it without comment in *Robbery Under Arms* (p. 293).

The Port Jackson word for a coward, *jerrun* (*jerran* or *jirrand* are more common later spellings), is used adjectivally in Aboriginal pidgin through to 1850 and possibly later. Thus Alexander Harris describes himself in 1847 as beginning to 'feel rather "jerran", as the blacks say (*i.e.*

---

[12] Ridley, *Kamilaroi, Dippil and Turrubul.*
[13] G. Tipsmill, 'The Snake', in Stewart and Keesing (ed.), *Old Bush Songs*, p. 33.

timorous)'.[14] But, again, this is not a word found much outside the context of pidgin.

The same is true of the intensive *murry*. Harris has one of the Aboriginal characters in *The Emigrant Family* speak of 'murry gourri jumbuc' (very fat sheep),[15] and the word is used in a similar context by a very unhappy missionary in 1824:

> To two Brothers of mine, these monsters exposed several pieces of human flesh, exclaiming as they smacked their lips and stroked their breasts, 'boodjerry patta! murry boodjerry!—fat as jimbuck!!' i.e. good food, very good, fat as mutton. There is no doubt of their cannibalism. Pray for me, and for them.[16]

This, incidentally, is the earliest use yet recorded of *jumbuck*, an Aboriginal pidgin word which has been rather fancifully derived from an Aboriginal word meaning 'the white mist preceding a shower, to which a flock of sheep bore a strong resemblance'.[17] This word, *dombar*, and *dombock*, 'a sheep', are both recorded in Gunther's vocabulary of the Wiradhuri language and Gunther indicates clearly that the two words are unrelated.[18] The most likely derivation of *jumbuck* is that suggested by Ridley, that the word is a corruption of 'jump-up'.[19]

Baal, bogie, budgeree, cobbra, jerran, and *murry* are all of Port Jackson origin and to them we can add a handful of words borrowed from other tribes as the settlers moved inland and along the coast from Sydney: *binghi*, 'brother', recorded north of Sydney and *bingy*, 'stomach', recorded at Bateman's Bay (near which it still occurs as a place-name), *yarraman*, 'horse', probably from Bateman's Bay, and *yakka* and *humpy*, from the Moreton Bay dialect. *Binghi* was given a new lease of life through its adoption

[14] *Settlers and Convicts*, p. 122.

[15] Vol. 2, p. 177.

[16] W. Walker to Secretary, Wesleyan Missionary Society, 26 January 1824.

[17] A. Meston, *Bulletin*, 18 April 1896.

[18] 'Grammar and Vocabulary of the Aboriginal Dialect called the Wirradhuri', in J. Fraser, *An Australian Language*.

[19] Ridley, *Kamilaroi and other Australian Languages*, p. 22.

by the *Bulletin*, but is not widely used now. *Bingy*, on the other hand, has passed into general colloquial speech, as has *yakka*, and both words are used in New Zealand as well as in Australia.

This group of words occurs first in the so-called Aboriginal pidgin which was used by the settlers to communicate with the Aborigines, a mixture of English and Aboriginal on which David Collins commented in 1796:

> Language indeed, is out of the question for at the time of writing this, nothing but a barbarous mixture of English with the Port Jackson dialect is spoken by either party; and it must be added that even in this the natives have the advantage, comprehending, with much greater aptness than we can pretend to, everything they hear us say.[20]

Nor would it seem that the English the Aborigines were acquiring as the other half of the mixture was of a very respectable character. Tench observed that the convicts were distinguished by their use of 'the flash or kiddy language' and that in courts of law 'an interpreter was frequently necessary to translate the deposition of the witness, and the defence of the prisoner'.[21] And, in 1827, Cunningham mentions the Billingsgate slang which the Aborigines used, adding that 'no white need think of competing with them in abuse or hard swearing, a constant torrent of which flows from their mouths as long as their antagonist remains before them. . . .'[22]

Evidence of the character of this 'mixture' is hard to obtain. It is unlikely that the recording of Aboriginal words in early letters or diaries will by itself give an accurate impression of their use in the speech of the colony. *Gin*, for example, occurs as early as 1791 in a passage of a letter to England describing an Aboriginal's 'gift of his thin Ding (wife)' to the Governor. This may suggest that the word was in general use among colonists in conversing with the Aborigines—or even among them-

20 *Account of the English Colony*, vol. 1, p. 544.
21 *Complete Account*, p. 207.
22 *Two Years in New South Wales*, vol. 2, p. 9.

selves—but it probably means no more than that the writer had heard or learnt a few words of the Port Jackson language and wanted to show them off in his correspondence. More reliable evidence of the currency of Aboriginal words among the colonists is that which gives an impression of speech rather than simply of words heard and recorded. There is, for example, a list of 'barbarisms' in the Hunter River language, 'words which have crept into use introduced by sailors, stockmen and others who have paid no attention to the aboriginal tongue'.[23] This was recorded by Threlkeld in 1834 and includes three non-Australian words, *gammon, piccaninny*, and *strike-a-light*, as well as a number of Port Jackson words which have since had a long period of general use: *baal, bogey, budgeree, carbon, 'large', gibber, gunyah, hielamon, jerran, mogo, pyalla, waddy*, and *woomera*. Also in the list is *kangaroo*. It seems reasonable to assume that these words derive from the 'barbarous mixture' to which Collins referred in 1796, and that the Hunter River Aborigines had learnt them from colonists moving north from Sydney.

Other writers, commenting on the language used by the Aborigines, support this impression. There appears to have developed in the Port Jackson area a 'third language', used for most communication between colonists and Aborigines and adopted by those colonists who moved inland or north and south along the coast from Sydney as an appropriate means of conversing with Aborigines, whether they spoke the Port Jackson language or not. Thus T. L. Mitchell, in his journal entry for 2 January 1832, describes an attempt at conversing with Aborigines in the Liverpool Plains district:

> The string of low slang words which the natives nearer the colony suppose to be our language, while our stockmen believe they speak theirs, was of no use here. In vain did Dawkins address them thus: *What for you jerran budgerry whitefellow? Whitefellow brother belongit to black fellow.*[24]

[23] L. E. Threlkeld, *An Australian Grammar*, Introduction.
[24] *Three Expeditions into the Interior of Eastern Australia*, vol. 1, p. 63.

J. D. Lang, in 1847, describes a similar situation in the Moreton Bay district:

> It is very difficult now to ascertain what are really the peculiar words of any particular dialect or language among the Aborigines in the Moreton Bay district—there is such a confusion of tongues especially in their intercourse with Europeans. A considerable number of words of the Sydney Aboriginal dialect known to the convicts or other white persons, in the earlier period of the Penal Settlement at Moreton Bay, were naturally enough made use of in attempting to hold communication with the black natives. These words, which were quite as unintelligible to the natives as the corresponding words in the vernacular of the white man would have been, were learned by the natives, and are now commonly used by them in conversing with Europeans as English words. Thus *corrobbory*, the Sydney word for a general assembly of natives, is now commonly used in that sense at Moreton Bay; but the original word there is *yanerville*. *Cabon*, great; *narang*, little; *boodgeree*, good; *myall*, wild native; etc. are all words of this description, supposed by natives to be English words, and by the Europeans to be Aboriginal words of the language of that district.[25]

Examples of this patois are rare, but the *Sydney Gazette*'s account on 2 January 1828 of the execution of an Aboriginal for the murder of a white man seems convincingly literal:

> He frequently said to one of the clergymen who occasionally visited him in his cell, 'All gammon white fellow pai-alla cabon gunyah, me tumble down white fellow.' It was all false that the white fellows said in the Court-house, that I killed the white fellow . . . on being told that it would be of no benefit to him to deny his guilt any longer as the white fellow was coming with the kurryjong, and that he must die, he shook his head and said, 'Kurryjong bail boodgeree', by which he seems to have meant, 'It is a sad thing to die in this way.' Mr. Threlkeld, who had been with him for some time, then

[25] *Cooksland*, p. 447.

left the cell, when turning to the clergyman who remained with him and exhibiting an appearance of
earnestness which he had not previously evinced, he said:
'Me like it pai-alla you gentleman.' I wish to speak to
you Sir. 'Bail Saturdey tumble down white fellow, bail
me tumble down white fellow—Tommy tumble down
white fellow, sit down Palabbala, bulla jin, like it me,
brother.' Neither Saturdey, nor Jingulo, nor myself
killed the white man; Tommy, a black fellow who lives
at Palabbala, (about thirty miles from Bathurst) and has
two jins, and is as like me as my brother, killed the
white fellow.

When the executioner had adjusted the rope, and was
about to pull the cap over his eyes, he exclaimed, with
a most pitiful expression of countenance, 'Murry me
jerran.' I am exceedingly afraid, and immediately after-
wards, casting his eyes wistfully around him, and giving
a melancholy glance at the apparatus of death, he said,
in a tone of deep feeling, which it was impossible to hear
without strong emotion, 'Bail more walk about,' meaning that his wanderings were over now (p. 2).

Less convincing than this passage but nonetheless indicative of the currency of 'pidgin' English are passages of
dialogue in descriptions of the colony of New South Wales
intended for English readers, in Dawson's *Present State of
Australia* (1831), for example:

'You hear, Massa? Black pellow cooee. Broder belonging
to me, massa: tit (sit) down here always'[26]

'I tumble down pickaninny here. . . . Belonging to
me all about, massa; pose you tit down here, I gib it to
you' ('Very well,' I said, 'I shall sit down here.') 'Budgeree' (very good), he replied, 'I gib it to you; . . .'[27]

Or in Harris's *Emigrant Family* (1849):

'Baal Englishman, me,' said Beck, 'Baal I like Englishman. That too much take away black fellow's land. That
too much, hunt away kangaroo, possum, fish. That

[26] Dawson, *Present State of Australia*, p. 11.
[27] Ibid., p. 12.

jumbuc (sheep) too much drink up all bardo (water).[28]

Initially, then, the sources of the pidgin were Port Jackson Aboriginal and the vulgar English of convicts and of the sailors who passed through Sydney, Collins's 'barbarous mixture', which spread through New South Wales and Queensland and which, though added to from later sources, formed the basis of the Australian pidgin used today. Thus, in a vocabulary of pidgin English, compiled in the north and west of Australia and published in Toronto in 1939, E. S. Sayer's *Pidgin English*, most of the words are corruptions of Standard English word-forms. But the majority of the Aboriginal words, like *cooee, corroboree, gin, gunyah, hielamon, myall, nulla nulla, waddy* and *warrigal*, are of Port Jackson origin. Other Aboriginal words, *bora, coolamon, goondie, humpy*, and *yarraman*, came from tribes in the Sydney and Moreton Bay districts and, like a number of words of English origin, *blackfellow, boy, debil-debil, mob, piccaninny, sit down*, 'stay', and *walkabout*, were in use before 1840.

From the early years of the colony, then, we can distinguish two classes of borrowings. A number of words were given an uncertain degree of permanence through being used in the colloquial speech of colonists and Aborigines, and these can be distinguished from a larger and more important group of words, *dingo, kangaroo, koala*, and *wallaby*, for example, words borrowed more or less deliberately to describe those features of Aboriginal life and of the flora and fauna of the country which were useful or interesting but for which there was no suitable English word.

The spread of this latter group was in the main no less rapid than that of the first. The distinctiveness of the kangaroo and its subsequent identification with Australia not unnaturally ensured the word's currency. But *boomerang*, first recorded in English in 1827, was used in Western Australia in 1832 in the definition of the word *kylie* (boomerang), and in 1834 was listed by Threlkeld in the Hunter River district, and by Lhotsky, in the Monaro

28 Vol. 2, p. 176.

district,[29] as a 'barbarism', a word introduced (presumably by a colonist) from one Aboriginal language into another. In some cases, particularly where two words, one English and one Aboriginal, were used for the same referent, the process of adoption was spread over a longer period. Words like *dingo, gunyah*, and *hielamon* are frequently found in conjunction with a descriptive synonym many years after their first recorded use in English. So Mundy, in 1852, refers to the 'dingo, warrigal or native dog',[30] and the coupling of *hielamon* and *shield, gunyah* and *bark hut* or *breakweather* is fairly common.

At the same time we find explorers and naturalists recording Aboriginal words for flora and fauna which have subsequently been used in English but seldom in a popular context. Thus the Aboriginal word *berigora* was adopted in 1827 as the scientific name for the hawk, *Falco berigora*, and there are a few other little-known names of birds and animals, *jerryang* and *potoroo*, for example, which are found fairly early.

Some idea of the extent and character of the borrowing from Aboriginal languages can be gained from the following list of words, all of which are found used in English before 1850. The largest group is that of names for animals, fish, birds, and insects: *berigora*, 'a brown hawk', *bettong*, 'a small kangaroo', *boobook, budgerigar, carbora*, 'a water worm', *cunjevoi*, 'a sedentary animal growth found on rocks', *dingo, jerryang*, 'a lorikeet', *kangaroo, koala, potoroo*, 'a kangaroo', *tandan*, 'a catfish', *wallaby, wallaroo, warrigal, wombat, wonga wonga*, 'a pigeon', *yarraman*, 'horse'. There are also, as one would expect, a number of names for trees and plants: *brigalow, burrawang*, 'a nut', *geebung, goborro*, 'a type of eucalypt', *kurrajong, mulga, quandong, waratah*, and *yarrah*.

A good proportion of the words are words associated with the way of life of the Aborigines, names for Aborigi-

---

[29] 'Some Remarks on a Short Vocabulary of the Natives of Van Diemen Land; and also of the Menero Downs in Australia', *Royal Geographical Society of London Journal*, vol. 9 (1839), pp. 157-62.

[30] *Our Antipodes*, vol. 1, p. 313.

nal customs, dwellings, implements, and people: *boomer-ang, coolamon,* 'a wooden dish', *corroboree, gin, gunyah, hielamon,* 'bark shield', *koradji,* 'priest', *mogo,* 'axe', *myall, nulla nulla, waddy,* and *woomera.* And there is the group of words borrowed into colloquial speech: *baal, binghi, bogey, budgeree, cobbra, cooee, gibber, jerran, jumbuck,* and *murry.*

These are all words borrowed from Aboriginal languages of New South Wales and to these we must add a few from the other settlements: *boobialla,* 'an acacia', and *lubra* from Tasmania; *borak, bunyip, leangle,* 'a club', *lerp,* 'a sweet secretion found on the leaves of the *Eucalyptus dumosa', lowan,* 'mallee-fowl', *mallee, mia mia, quamby,* 'hut', and *tuan,* 'a flying squirrel' from Victoria; *dilly, bunya bunya, humpy, kipper,* 'young man', and *yakka* from Queensland; *kylie* and *wilga,* 'red ochre', from Western Australia; and *wurley,* 'hut', from South Australia.

This makes up about one-third of all the Aboriginal words which have been recorded in use in Australian English. The list will almost certainly be extended by sub-sequent investigations, but it is unlikely that its character will be greatly changed. The major categories, names for flora and fauna and for features of Aboriginal life, are those in which we would most expect borrowings in the early years of the settlement and those which, if we extend the period to take account of all Aboriginal borrowings which are found in use in Australian English during the nine-teenth century, continue, as the following selective lists show, to be of the greatest importance.

1 TREES AND PLANTS

bangalow	coolibah
belah	geebung
boobialla	gidgee
boree	goborro
brigalow	gunyang
bunya bunya	jarrah
burrawang	karri
coobah	kurrajong

lerp	quandong
mallee	tuart
mulga	wandoo
murrnong	waratah
myall	wilga
nardoo	yarrah
pituri	yarran

Not unnaturally the colonists sought from the Aborigines the names of trees and plants which they saw them using for some purpose or other, and the names of those trees and plants which were in some way particularly striking. So there are a number of Aboriginal words, some of them practically obsolete now, which were borrowed during the early years of settlement as labels for foodstuffs used by the Aborigines. One of these is *bunya bunya* or, as a Moreton Bay missionary described it in 1843, 'the celebrated Bunga Bunga tree', the cone of which he found highly prized by the Aborigines, and perhaps the most nutritious natural production of Australia.[31] There is also *burwan*, or *burrawang*, a nut which, according to one visitor to the colony of New South Wales, was much relished by the natives;[32] *bangalow*, a palm tree, the young leaves of which were eaten by the Aborigines; *geebung* (also *gibong* or *jibbong*) or native plum; *gunyang* or *kangaroo apple*, found in Gippsland; *lerp*, a sweet secretion found on the leaves of the mallee in north-west Victoria; *murrnong*, an edible root found in Victoria; and, perhaps most interesting of all, *nardoo* and *pituri*, both of which first became known as a result of the Burke and Wills expedition in 1860-1. Burke, Wills, and King, returning from Cooper's Creek, their supplies exhausted, were forced to follow the example of the Aborigines and gather the seeds of the *nardoo*, from which a rough sort of flour could be made and baked into cakes. The Aborigines also gave them *pituri* (or *pitchery*), a drug made from the powdered leaves and twigs of a small tree, *Duboisia hopwoodii*. King described it thus:

[31] J. Gregor, Journal, 23 August 1843.
[32] Cunningham, *Two Years in New South Wales*, vol. 1, p. 221.

After chewing it for a few minutes I felt quite happy and perfectly indifferent about my position, in fact much the same effect as might be produced by two pretty stiff nobblers of brandy. After chewing it the natives do not throw it away but place it behind the ear, much in the same style as a sailor places his quid in his hat, until it has lost all goodness. Offering this pitchery pill to a stranger is the greatest expression of amity which, however, we did not at first understand and felt rather disgusted than otherwise when they used to press upon our acceptance their nasty dirty-looking balls of chewed grass, as it appeared to be.[33]

Useful in a different way was the *kurrajong* (or *currajong*). Now used only as the popular name of a tree, *kurrajong* was first recorded by Southwell in 1788 as the Port Jackson word for fishing line, and it seems in the first half of the nineteenth century to have been used indiscriminately of any fibrous bark which could be made into rope and, by association, of any tree or shrub which carried such a bark. The following quotations illustrate the variety of uses to which the kurrajong was put:

Many parts are covered with a new hibiscus, which the natives use as flax for making their nets and for other purposes. This plant is much superior to the carradgan, which is of the same species.[34]

. . . they strangled him by a narrow strip of bark, called by the natives, curryjung, and then threw him into the water; . . .[35]

(he dreamed) that God pulled him in at a window with curryjong, (that is a cord so called because they make use of the bark of a tree of that name for the general purposes of twine or rope).[36]

At least two other words are used in the same way. *Mulga* is recorded in the 1830s as the name for a weapon,

[33] A. Moorehead, *Cooper's Creek*, p. 118.
[34] King to Portland, 21 August 1801, *H.R.A.*, vol. III, p. 179 ('Paterson's Journal' for 21 August 1801).
[35] Dawson, op. cit., p. 43.
[36] W. Watson, Journal, 20 June 1833.

a shield made from mulga wood, but it is used also as the popular name for various species of acacia, properly for *Acacia aneura*. And *gidgee* (also *gidya* or *giddea*), first recorded in 1838, in a vocabulary of the Wiradhuri language, with the meaning 'a little tree',[37] is used both of a species of acacia, *A. homalophylla*, and of a long spear made from the wood of this tree.

A further group of trees would seem to have been distinctive not for their usefulness but for their appearance. Pride of place here goes to the *waratah*, described in 1793 'by common consent both of Europeans and Natives' as 'the most magnificent plant which the prolific soil of New Holland affords'.[38] The *myall* (*A. pendula*) was hailed by a later visitor as 'the most picturesque tree of New South Wales',[39] and *mallee*, which has given its name to the district where it is abundant, was equally distinctive, if in a different way.

In some instances the same tree acquired several names, each borrowed from a different Aboriginal language. Thus *A. pendula*, called *myall* in the eastern part of New South Wales, was known by the Kamilaroi name, *boree*, in the west and south-west, and also by the Wiradhuri name, *yarran*. *Goborro*, the earliest Aboriginal name for *Eucalyptus microtheca*, popularly known also as *dwarf*, or *flooded box*, and *swamp gum*, was current in western New South Wales in the first half of the century, but could not compete with the Kamilaroi name, *coolabah* (or *coolibah*), probably because of the currency *coolibah* found in ballads and popular songs. A word like *coolibah* which, for some reason or other, achieves general currency, obviously has a far better chance of survival than a word which remains current only in a particular region. Thus *boobialla*, a Tasmanian word for *A. longifolia*, is not well known on the mainland and, although the names of the Western Australian hardwoods, *karri* and *jarrah*, have become

[37] Gunther, op. cit.

[38] J. E. Smith, *Specimen of Botany of New Holland*, p. 19 (from Morris, *Austral English*).

[39] J. O. Balfour, *Sketch of New South Wales* (1845), p. 38 (from Morris, *Austral English*).

fairly well established throughout Australia, the names of other Western Australian trees like *tuart* and *wandoo* are little known.

2 ANIMALS

bettong	potoroo
brumby	quokka
bunyip	tamma
dingo	tuan
kangaroo	wallaby
koala	wallaroo
numbat	warrigal
paddymelon	wombat

Of these names for animals, the Western Australian contingent has retained for the most part only a regional currency. *Numbat,* the name of a banded anteater, and *tamma,* the name of a kangaroo, have continued in Western Australian use from the earliest days of the settlement, but only *quokka,* the name of a small wallaby found on Rottnest Island, has achieved a wider currency, and this because the animal itself is something of a curiosity.

Other words from this list are rarely used now: *bettong,* the Port Jackson name for a small kangaroo, which survives in the name of the genus *Bettongia;* *potoroo,* the Port Jackson name for a rare kangaroo-rat; and *tuan,* a Victorian Aboriginal name for a flying squirrel, a word which Kingsley used in *Geoffrey Hamlyn* as the name of a bushranger who habitually struck by night. *Paddymelon* (or *pademelon*), the popular name of a group of small wallabies, is more common. The word is usually described as a corruption of the Port Jackson word for kangaroo, *patagorang,* but King, in a list of species of kangaroo found at Port Jackson in 1827, records both *patagorang* and *pademalion* without suggesting that they refer to the same species.[40] It is probable, therefore, that *paddymelon* is a quite unrelated word from the Port Jackson or an adjacent vocabulary.

[40] P. P. King, *Narrative of a Survey of the Intertropical and Western Coasts of Australia,* vol. 2, pp. 632-7.

Dingo and *warrigal* are both Port Jackson words in origin and both appear to have meant much the same thing to the Aborigines. But, whereas *dingo*, apart from its later figurative use in reference to a person who displays some of the characteristics of the animal, has always meant a particular sort of dog, *Canis familiaris dingo*, *warrigal* has had a much wider range of meanings. It is indicative of the spread of this word that it was recorded in the vocabulary of a north Victorian Aboriginal language in 1859 with the meaning 'ferocious, savage, wild',[41] and it seems to have been used during the nineteenth century fairly indiscriminately as a synonym for *wild* and more specifically of wild Aborigines, or *myalls*, dogs and horses.

Wallaby and *wombat* are also Port Jackson words and were both in use from the earliest days of the colony. *Wallaroo*, first recorded somewhat later, in 1827,[42] is probably from one of the languages used immediately to the north of Sydney. All these animals were, of course, a source of great interest when first discovered, not least the *koala* (or, as the *Oxford English Dictionary* still enters it, *koolah*). First reports came in 1798 of 'another animal which the natives call a cullawine, which much resembles the stoths [sloths] of America',[43] but it was not until 1802 that 'portions of a monkey (in the native language, "Colo")'[44] were brought in for examination. A word similar to *cullawine* is recorded by Threlkeld, to the north of Sydney in 1826,[45] and is probably from a different language. The earliest transcriptions of *koala—colo, cola, coloo*, and *coola*—are all of two syllables and it is probable that the modern trisyllabic pronunciation is based on a misreading.

Neither of the two words remaining, *brumby* and *bunyip*, is a New South Wales word and each is, in its own way, something of a mystery. *Brumby* is probably

[41] Smyth, op. cit., vol. 2, pp. 133-53.

[42] King, op. cit.

[43] 'Anonymous Account of a Journey to the Blue Mountains', *H.R.N.S.W.*, vol. iii, p. 821.

[44] 'Barrallier's Journal', *H.R.N.S.W.*, vol. v, App. A, p. 759.

[45] L. E. Threlkeld, Papers.

I

derived from a Queensland Aboriginal word *booramby*, meaning 'wild', but popular etymologies are a long time a-dying and there is still current the theory, first recorded by Morris, that in the early day of the colony

> a Lieutenant Brumby, who was on the staff of one of the Governors, imported some very good horses, and that some of their descendants being allowed to run wild became the ancestors of the wild horses of New South Wales and Queensland.[46]

The mystery of *bunyip* is not linguistic. *Bunyip* is a north Victorian Aboriginal word for a legendary creature, described in 1848 as 'of amphibious character, inhabiting deep rivers and permanent water-holes, having a round head, an elongated neck, with a body and tail resembling an ox'.[47] Investigations have not proved the existence of such a monster, nor is there any confirmation of an alternative theory, that bunyips were nothing more than strayed cattle frequenting and perhaps becoming bogged in waterholes.

One advantage, as G. C. Mundy pointed out in 1852, has arisen from the long-deferred discovery of the true nature of the bunyip: 'a new and strong word was adopted into the Australian vocabulary: Bunyip became, and remains a Sydney synonyme for *impostor, pretender, humbug*, and the like'.[48] Particularly in the expression *bunyip aristocracy*, used of Wentworth's 1853 scheme for an Upper House with hereditary peers, *bunyip* was, in fact, an amusing and forceful addition to the vocabulary.

3 FISH

barramundi	teraglin
cunjevoi	toopong
luderick	wirrah
morwong	wobegong
nannygai	wollomai
tarwhine	yabby

[46] *Austral English.*
[47] W. Westgarth, *Australia Felix*, p. 391.
[48] Mundy, *Our Antipodes*, vol. 2, p. 19.

Names of fish, like those of other fauna, are likely, unless the fish is of peculiar distinction, to be restricted in use to particular areas. Thus *luderick*, a Gippsland Aboriginal name for 'blackfish', *morwong* (the New Zealand *tarakihi*), *nannygai*, *tarwhine*, *teraglin* and *wirrah* are all names of fish found on the east coast of Australia. *Barramundi* (or *burramundi*) is a North Queensland fish which has become rather more widely known, *toopong* (or *tupong*) is a fish found on the southern coast of Australia, and *yabby* is the name used in most of New South Wales, Victoria, and Tasmania for a freshwater crayfish. (It is used also on the northern New South Wales and Queensland coast for a marine crustacean.)

Wobegong and *wollomai* are, unfortunately, not much used now. *Wobegong* (or *woe-begone* as it was once written) is an Aboriginal name for the carpet shark and *wollomai* the Port Jackson word for 'snapper'. Both have gone out of use in face of the general currency of the better-known names. *Cunjevoi* is again little used, not because of the prevalence of any alternative popular name (i.e. *sea squirt*) but because the animal itself, a small, sedentary growth found on east coast rocks at low tide, attracts the attention of a relatively small number of people. Restricted as its currency may be, it goes back at least to 1821.[49]

4 BIRDS

berigora	galah
boobook	gang-gang
brolga	jerryang
budgerigar	kookaburra
bulln-bulln	lowan
corella	wonga wonga
currawong	

Several of these birds' names are clearly onomatopoeic, imitations made by the Aborigines of the bird's call, and

---

[49] S. Leigh to Secretary, Wesleyan Missionary Society. Leigh records *conguwa*, 'a kind of living fungus, which at certain Seasons they detach from the Rocks on the Sea Shore'. Threlkeld, in *An Australian Grammar* (1834), records *kunje-wy*.

this may help to account for their adoption into English. *Boobook*, for instance, the Port Jackson Aboriginal name for an owl, is obviously a close relation of the more commonly used *mopoke* (or *morepork*). Although the birds to which these names refer are properly quite distinct, the sounds they make are similar. As *boobook* is the older of the two, being recorded in the earliest glossaries of the Port Jackson language, it is possible that *mopoke* is a variant of this or, as seems more likely, a name separately derived from the bird's call by the colonists.

Currawong, again, is imitative. It is recorded in Hunter's vocabulary of 1790 as *terrawana*, the Port Jackson word for magpie, and by Threlkeld, north of Sydney in 1826, as *cur-ow-ung*.[50] Threlkeld also provides, in the same glossary, the earliest record of *kookaburra*. Oddly enough, although it was found as early as this, *kookaburra* did not come into general currency in Australian English until towards the end of the nineteenth century. The bird was certainly not rare as visitors to the colony comment on its call with great frequency; but the settlers chose rather to call it by any one of several descriptive compounds, *laughing jackass* and *settler's clock* being the most common.

Several of the other words in this list have, like *kookaburra*, remained in occasional use during the nineteenth century as alternatives to more generally current names, *brolga*, for instance, for the *native companion* (a crane), *bulln-bulln*, a Victorian Aboriginal name for the 'lyre-bird', and *lowan*, for the 'mallee-fowl'. *Gang-gang* (or *gangan*), the name of a cockatoo, and *wonga wonga*, the name of a pigeon, are New South Wales words and have both been in use since the early part of the century. *Galah*, the name of a widely distributed pink and grey cockatoo, is a somewhat later borrowing, well-established in this sense, and interesting for the development of a second, figurative sense, 'fool or simpleton', familiar in Australian slang and presumably derived from the bird's behaviour. *Corella*, again the name of a cockatoo, is interesting in a

[50] Papers.

different way, as an example of a word which has had an ingenious classical etymology provided for it. Morris saw the word as a diminutive of late Latin *cora*, 'a girl or doll', and this suggestion has been adopted by later dictionaries. It seems far more likely that the word is of Aboriginal origin, derived from the Port Jackson *ca-rall*, 'black cockatoo', recorded in Hunter's vocabulary, and that the modern form *corella* has been influenced by the word's supposed Latin origin.

5   GRUBS, FLIES, ETC.

bardi	korrumburra
carbora	witchetty

Of these few words only *witchetty* has any general currency. Like *bardi*, which is a Western Australian word, it is the name of an edible grub valued by the Aborigines. *Carbora* and *korrumburra* survive only as place-names or parts of place-names. *Korrumburra* (or *korumburra*), the name of a biting fly of the genus *Tabanus*, is also the name of a Victorian country town, *carbora*, the name of a water worm that eats into timber, possibly the source of the first part of *Cabramatta*, an area which, according to J. D. Lang in 1847, abounded in the *carbora*. Lang described the worm as 'resembling the contents of a marrow-bone',[51] but David Collins, in 1798, found it even more distasteful. He described

a piece of water-soken wood (part of a branch of a tree) full of holes, the lodgement of a large worm, named by them cah-bro, and which they extract and eat; but nothing could be more offensive than the smell of both the worm and its habitation. There is a tribe of natives dwelling inland, who, from the circumstance of their eating these loathsome worms are named Cah-bro-gal.[52]

6   PHYSICAL FEATURES

billabong	gilgai
gibber	namma

[51] Lang, *Cooksland*, p. 444.
[52] Collins, op. cit., vol. 1, p. 558.

The oldest of these words, or the one that has been in use in English for longest, is *gibber,* the Port Jackson Aboriginal word for a stone. *Gibber* seems now to be used mainly of largish stones or boulders lying in desert country, as in *gibber-plain,* but its early use was less specific. Alexander Harris, in 1847, uses *gibber* of an overhanging rock, alongside a river, where a man could take shelter,[53] and a similar sort of hollow or cave is described in 1850 by G. F. Angas, who learnedly supplies his own etymology:

> At Port Aiken and in Middle Harbour they are found in caves, formed by projecting masses of rock, called by the natives 'Giber Gunyah'; i.e. stone or rock house. Thus, a black fellow, on his first arrival in Sydney, seeing a stone house exclaimed, 'Ah! white fellow too in giber gunyah!' The term is of eastern origin, as appears from the derivation. *Giber* (in Arabic), a hump on a camel's back; a rock. *Giber,* altar, Gibraltar. *Gunn* (in Arabic), preserving; covering; shading from the sun; a veil; court or middle of a house.[54]

Gilgai (also *ghilgai* or *gilgie*), a New South Wales word, and *namma,* a Western Australian word, both refer to saucer-shaped depressions in the ground which hold water. Morris derived *namma* from a Queensland word *ngumma,* 'a breast', but this raises difficulties; the probable derivation is from a Western Australian word recorded in 1842: *amar, ngamar,* 'a hole or pool of water in a rock'.[55] *Billabong,* similarly, has fallen prey to amateur etymologists. The most common explanation of the word is that given by Morris, who traces both elements of the compound to the Wiradhuri dialect of New South Wales, *billa* being the Wiradhuri word for 'river', and *bong,* or *bung* meaning 'dead'. *Bong* is, in fact, not from Wiradhuri but from a Queensland Aboriginal language: it occurs, for instance, in the name of the Brisbane suburb Humpy-bong in the 1840s and, perhaps influenced by the English slang word

---

[53] *Settlers and Convicts,* p. 87.

[54] *Savage Life and Scenes in Australia and New Zealand,* Appendix.

[55] Moore, *A Descriptive Vocabulary.*

bung, is found fairly widely in Aboriginal pidgin in the second half of the century.

That *billabong* is a Wiradhuri compound is clear from the earliest recorded uses of the word by the explorer T. L. Mitchell and from its appearance in a manuscript vocabulary of Wiradhuri compiled by a missionary stationed in the Wellington Valley in 1838. Mitchell not infrequently found difficulty in identifying physical features named by earlier explorers and so made a point himself of recording the Aboriginal names of rivers and hills in the country he passed through. Twice in his journal for 1836 he mentions the name *Billibang*, in both places as the Aboriginal name of the river now known as the Bell. This is supported by Gunther's vocabulary, in which *billabang* is given as the 'native name of the Bell River' and as the name for the 'Constellation called Milky Way'.[56] What the word meant to the Aborigines is not clear, though *billa* certainly meant 'water'. It is possible that the termination -*bang* derives from Wiradhuri *biang*, 'many'.

Mitchell's description of the Bell, 'a small watercourse, then dry and named Billibang, [which] skirts the eastern side of the hill, and then enters that branch of the Lachlan which we were upon',[57] suggests the English meaning of *billabong*. The probable development of the word's meaning between 1836 and 1860 is in three stages. Initially meaning the Bell River only, *billabong* came to be used of 'billabong country', country characterized by dried-out creek-beds and waterholes and, by 1862, was used of any dry creek or river. Thus W. Landsborough, describing the Macadam River in the far north of Australia, writes:

> In the south, such a creek as the Macadam is termed a *billy-bonn* from the circumstance of the water carrier returning from it with his pitcher (*billy*) empty (*bong*, literally *dead*).[58]

[56] The Native Dialect Wirradurri, spoken in the Wellington District, etc., 1838.

[57] *Three Expeditions to the Interior of Eastern Australia*, vol. 2, p. 20.

[58] *Exploration of Australia* (1862), p. 30 (from Morris, *Austral English*).

It was Landsborough's comment, perhaps, which led Sidney J. Baker to derive *billy,* almost certainly a Scottish dialectal word, from the Aboriginal *billa.* Certainly it is evidence of the early acceptance of the theory that *billabong* was made up of two elements and meant 'dead water'.

7 WEAPONS AND IMPLEMENTS

boomerang	mogo
coolamon	nulla nulla
dilly	waddy
hielamon	wirri
kylie	woomera
leangle	

It is understandable that the settlers, in their curiosity to learn as much about the inhabitants of New South Wales as they could, quickly learnt the names of the strange-looking weapons with which they were armed. *Hielamon,* 'bark shield', *mogo,* 'stone hatchet', *nulla nulla,* 'wooden club', *waddy,* 'stick or club', and *woomera,* 'throwing stick', are all Port Jackson Aboriginal words recorded in the earliest vocabularies of that language and subsequently adopted by the settlers. In one or two cases the form of the word, once borrowed, has been changed. The initial *h* of *hielamon,* for instance, is a later English addition and the pronunciation of *nulla nulla,* first recorded by David Collins as *gnal-lung-ul-la,* has fortunately been simplified.

The origin of *waddy* or, more accurately, its relation to English *wood* has given rise to some discussion. Baker, tracing the word back to 1804, describes it as 'an aboriginal pidgin corruption of "wood", used originally for a wooden club or stick',[59] and this is admitted as a possibility by Morris, the *Oxford English Dictionary*, and *Webster's*. But the word is first recorded in 1788 by Southwell, in his vocabulary of the Port Jackson language, and this occurrence, before any real contact had been made with the Aborigines, argues strongly for an Aboriginal origin. It would seem that here, as in the case of *billabong,* Baker

[59] *Australian Language,* p. 193.

has been misled by the similarity of form of two quite unrelated words.

Of the other words for weapons in this list two, *leangle*, 'a club', and *wirri*, 'a throwing stick', are Victorian, both coming from the Gippsland area, and one, *kylie*, is Western Australian. *Kylie*, a *boomerang*, is first found in a vocabulary compiled by Scott Nind in 1832 as '*curl*, curled stick or boomerang of Sydney'.[60] The description is interesting, for it is only a few years earlier, in 1827, that *boomerang* is found for the first time in English, described again as a Port Jackson word.[61] What is puzzling is that the word occurs in none of the earlier vocabularies and in none of the earlier descriptions of the Aborigines. Threlkeld, it is true, records *boomarring* in a manuscript vocabulary compiled to the north of Sydney in 1826 but, in his 1834 vocabulary, *boomerang* is listed as a barbarism introduced into the Awabakal language by the settlers.[62] These occurrences indicate that the word was in use in the area but are of little help in tracking down its origin.

One possibility is that the word is a corruption or variant of *womurrang*, recorded by Collins in 1798 in his vocabulary of the Port Jackson language. Collins defines *wommurang* as 'a club', but what appears to be the same word, this time spelt *wamareen*, is used under an illustration of a boomerang by S. Leigh in a letter to the Secretary of the Wesleyan Missionary Society in 1821.

Of the two words remaining, *coolamon*, the Wiradhuri word for a hollowed out knot of wood, used mostly for carrying water, has achieved relatively little currency in English, whereas *dilly*, especially in the tautologous form *dilly bag*, has passed into common use. *Dilly* is probably a Queensland word, and was used originally of a small plaited grass bag used by the Aborigines. Now any small

---

[60] S. Nind, 'Vocabulary of the Language of the Aborigines of Western Australia', *Royal Geographical Society of London Journal*, vol. 1 (1832); later in N. Ogle, *The Colony of Western Australia*, pp. 71-3.

[61] King, op. cit.

[62] MS. vocabulary (1826), in Papers; *An Australian Grammar*.

bag used for holding odds and ends may, especially in country districts, be called a *dilly bag*.

8 DWELLINGS

gundy	mia mia
gunyah	quamby
humpy	wurley

These six words are all from different Aboriginal languages and all refer to the same thing, the roughly-constructed bark shelter of the Aboriginal, described by Dawson in 1830 as a small hut

> supported by three forked sticks (about three feet long) brought together at the top in triangular form: the two sides toward the wind are covered by long sheets of bark, the third is always left open to the wind.[63]

Their use in English demonstrates again the readiness of the settlers to borrow the word immediately to hand and the frequency with which this acquired a local currency. Thus, although the Port Jackson word, *gunyah*, had been in use in English very early and by the 1830s was fairly widely used, synonyms were borrowed in several of the other settlements. *Gundy* is an inland New South Wales word, borrowed from the Wiradhuri language and first used in English in the Wellington Valley; *quamby* and *mia mia* are both Victorian, *quamby* appearing briefly in the Port Phillip district in the 1840s and *mia mia* becoming more generally current. *Humpy* is a Queensland Aboriginal word, coming into use in the 1840s in the form *umpee*. Like *hielamon* it has acquired an initial *h*, in this case possibly because the appearance of the Aboriginal hut has suggested the English word *hump*. *Wurley*, the last of the group, is South Australian.

In only one or two cases have the meanings of these words been extended. *Gunyah*, restricted now to its original meaning, experienced a period of expansion during the forties and fifties and was used of a goldminer's

---

[63] *Present State of Australia*, p. 171.

shack or stockman's hut, as well as in the compound
gibber-gunyah.

Mia mia was similarly used on the Victorian goldfields,
either of the prospector's rude hut (or *wigwam,* as it was
occasionally called) or of a shelter erected over the shaft
opening. This would seem also to be the origin of the
New Zealand *mai mai* or *mi mi,* a duck-shooter's blind.
Humpy, of course is widely used, not simply of an Aboriginal's shelter but of any rudely constructed hut.

9 CEREMONIES AND PEOPLE

bora	koradji
boyla	lubra
corroboree	myall
gin	warrigal
kipper	

Several of these words, notably *bora,* 'a rite of initiation',
kipper, used of a youth who has passed through such a
rite, and *boyla* and *koradji,* 'an aboriginal medicine-man
or witchdoctor', are used only in their original and specific
senses. The others have all passed into general colloquial
speech, acquiring meanings which are in some cases
generalized, in others figurative. *Corroboree,* for instance,
was mostly used, either as a noun or a verb, in its original
sense of 'a dance, sacred, festive, or warlike', but several,
albeit shortlived, figurative usages emerged, the word
being used of mosquitoes, which 'corroboreed with un-
mitigated ardour'[64] and of water boiling.[65] By the end of
the century two further figurative meanings had become
fairly common and *corroboree* was used in colloquial
speech of a social gathering or public meeting, and of a
noise or disturbance.

Gin and *lubra* are used of Aboriginal women and
occasionally, though only in slang and never as a compli-
ment, of women generally. *Gin* is a Port Jackson word
and was current very early. It had obvious possibilities for

[64] C. P. Hodgson, *Reminiscences of Australia,* p. 257.
[65] A. C. Grant, *Bush Life in Queensland* (1881), vol. 1, p. 43 (from
Morris, *Austral English*).

the amateur etymologist and several visitors to the colony had no hesitation in pronouncing it Greek. Others were more careful. Thus C. P. Hodgson, in *Reminiscences of Australia,* describes *gin* as 'the term applied to the native female Blacks'. 'Not', he adds, 'from any attachment to the spirit of that name, but from some (to me) unknown derivation.'[66] *Lubra,* less commonly used than *gin,* is Tasmanian in origin and was, up till about 1850, restricted mainly to Tasmania and Victoria. In the latter half of the century it became, like *gin,* a part of general Aboriginal pidgin.

Myall and *warrigal* also have similar meanings in modern English although, in the Port Jackson language from which they both come, their meanings were distinct and quite unrelated. *Warrigal,* the Port Jackson word for a large dog, was used by the settlers as a synonym for *dingo* and thence, by transference, for a wild horse (though the more common term was *brumby*) and an uncivilized Aborigine. *Myall* meant originally 'a stranger, an aboriginal from another tribe', but it quickly acquired new connotations. In 1832, for instance, T. L. Mitchell writes of a tribe glorying in the name of 'Myall', 'which the natives nearer to the colony apply in terror and abhorrence to the "wild blackfellows", to whom they attribute the most savage propensities'.[67] It is in the sense foreshadowed here, 'a wild or uncivilized aboriginal', that *myall* was used mostly in the pidgin of Queensland and the Northern Territory. From this the word has come, in some parts of the country, to be used more generally as a synonym for 'wild'. The connection between this sense and *myall* as a popular name for *Acacia pendula* is uncertain, but it is not improbable that the tree was so named either because it was first found in inland country inhabited by 'myall blacks' or because the wood of the tree was used by the 'myalls' for making certain weapons.

Borrowings from Aboriginal languages, then, fall into a number of clearly defined categories. One small group of

[66] *Reminiscences,* p. 80.
[67] *Three Expeditions into the Interior . . . ,* vol. 1, pp. 192-3.

words passed into the Aboriginal pidgin used by convicts and settlers to communicate with the Aborigines, but all the other words—names of flora and fauna, features of the landscape, or words relating to the way of life of the Aborigines—were accepted generally into Australian English. Many were borrowed early, the settlers naturally seeking and adopting an Aboriginal name for something with which they saw the Aborigines were familiar. Once borrowed they have tended to remain 'fixed' labels: a few words have developed figurative meanings but most are used today with meanings as specific as when they were first recorded.

Their future remains uncertain. Just as many of the American borrowings from the Indian languages have become localized in use or obsolete, so in Australian English the number generally current has dwindled, a recent survey showing that not more than forty of the words discussed here are at all widely known.[68] This undoubtedly results in part from the sort of contact Australians have had with Aborigines, and the depressed state of the Aboriginal today; but we must take into account also the scattered distribution of indigenous flora and fauna and the haphazardness with which, in different parts of the country, different names were bestowed by the settlers. A move towards uniformity probably meant a move towards English names which were descriptive and could more clearly indicate similarities and relations.

[68] W. S. Ramson, *The Currency of Aboriginal Words in Australian English.*

7

Borrowings from American English

THERE ARE a number of words common to American and Australian English of the nineteenth century which are not generally used in the British Isles. Most of these are borrowings. Australians quickly borrowed from the miners and adventurers who flocked from California to the Australian goldfields in the 1850s, bringing with them new methods and equipment for extracting alluvial gold. Similarly, the Australians who went to California in 1849 and 1850 and the American miners who returned to the United States in the 1850s and 1860s took with them a vocabulary of Australian English from which American borrowed: the verb *to buck*, recorded in Australia some twenty years earlier than in the United States, is one example.

But there are some words recorded in both American and Australian English which presumably, as there is no evidence of borrowing, have a common British slang or dialectal origin. Regional dialect *buster*, 'something very large', is probably the source of American *buster*, 'a spree', found as early as 1831, and Australian *buster*, 'a sudden, heavy wind', recorded in 1852; *dubersome*, 'doubtful', *to fall*, 'to fell a tree', *to nip*, 'to steal', and *to roust*, 'to disturb', are all words from English regional dialects recorded in both American and Australian English. The history of *run*, 'a tract of grazing land', demonstrates even more clearly this process of independent borrowing into the two colonial dialects. Probably of Yorkshire origin, *run* occurs commonly in Australian English from the 1820s, but once only, in an isolated occurrence dated 1658,

in American English.[1] *Shicer* (American *shyster*) and
spieler are used in the United States and in Australia with
slightly different meanings, and forms of both words are
recorded in nineteenth-century English slang (see p. 160
below).

We may expect to find, then, a number of instances in
the slang and colloquial vocabularies of American and
Australian English, as well as in occupational vocabularies, of words which do not occur in standard British
English (which therefore may not have been recorded by
the *Oxford English Dictionary*), but which have been
borrowed separately into American and Australian English
from British slang or regional dialect use. It would be
wrong to think of similarities of this sort as an indication
of either American influence on Australian English or
Australian on American. Nor should we too readily draw
conclusions (as Baker does)[2] about the histories of words
which are at present recorded earlier in American English
than they are in Australian. The historical information in
Morris and Baker is much less complete than that in
Mathews's *Dictionary of Americanisms* or Craigie and
Hulbert's *Dictionary of American English*.

Early contacts between Americans and Australians were
not of the sort to encourage linguistic borrowing.[3] American sealers and whalers called repeatedly at Port Jackson
from 1800 on and traders, speculators in the rum traffic,
or merchants bound for China, were of some importance
to the economy of New South Wales between 1800 and
1814; but the first United States consul in Sydney was not
appointed until 1839 and early trading contacts, tempor-
arily checked by the 1812-14 war and by subsequent trade
restrictions imposed by the British government, were
irregular. Fear of American competition to the British
whaling fleets caused Governor King to prohibit the
American use of Port Jackson as a base in 1804, and,

[1] Mathews, *A Dictionary of Americanisms on Historical Principles.*

[2] *The Australian Language*, p. 277.

[3] *Tomahawk* was used early to describe an Aboriginal's club: the
word was in general English use in this sense but may have been
borrowed directly from American seamen.

though American whalers continued to call at Sydney, it is unlikely that their crews or the traders' crews would have mixed with the settlers to any great extent.[4]

As early as 1804 colonial sealers were employed by American captains,[5] and Dakin states that, particularly between 1830 and 1860, Americans 'deliberately sought crews mixed in nationality as well as in colour', in the belief that 'there was less chance of mutual agreement and mutiny with such a heterogeneous crowd'.[6] It is unlikely that the language used by these crews, probably a 'pidgin' English with affiliations to that used by seamen in New Zealand, Australia, and the Pacific Islands, would have contributed to the vocabulary of the colony.

The discovery of gold in Victoria brought the first significant influx of Americans: 16,000 miners, some of them returning Australians, arrived from the Californian goldfields between 1852 and 1856,[7] bringing with them mining terms which were introduced into Australian English.[8] It is probable that non-technical words were borrowed at the same time.

From the middle to the end of the nineteenth century traders and tourists moved freely between America and Australia, with the consequent possibility of words being borrowed from one country into another. We would expect, and indeed find, a growing number of colloquialisms of American origin in late nineteenth-century Australian English. In this chapter I have attempted to define two groups of additions to the 'standard' vocabulary of Aus-

---

[4] See G. Greenwood, *Early American-Australian Relations from the Arrival of the Spaniards in America to the Close of 1830*; also L. G. Churchward, 'The American Contribution to the Victorian Gold Rush', *Victorian Historical Magazine*, vol. 19 (1941-2), pp. 85-95; W. J. Dakin, *Whalemen Adventurers*; and a useful article in the *Australian Encyclopaedia*, vol. 1.

[5] Greenwood, op. cit., p. 84.

[6] Op. cit., p. 4.

[7] Churchward, op. cit., p. 90.

[8] More than 800 Australians entered California in 1849; most of these returned in 1851. See W. Levi, *American-Australian Relations*, pp. 37-8.

tralian English: the first a small but interesting group of words of American origin which, contrary to all expectations, were borrowed into Australian English before 1850; the second a larger group of words, those associated with the discovery and mining of gold, borrowed during the 1850s.

The words borrowed before 1850 are all from the one area of usage: four of them, *block, location, section,* and *township,* were used with specific senses in the surveying of land for settlement, and the remaining four, *bush, bushranger* (meaning 'woodsman', 'bushman'), *landshark,* and *squatter,* belong to the same context. It is unlikely that these were borrowed from American traders, sealers, or whalers in Sydney, as they were all in general use early, in the formal correspondence of officials as well as in more colloquial contexts. In fact their early occurrence in letters from London suggests that these words were borrowed via Whitehall, that British colonial administrators, familiar with American practice, used them in planning the extension of settlement in New South Wales.

Evidence which further supports this thesis is the use of *planter* for *settler* in a paragraph of the Instructions to Governor Hunter, which defines the area to be laid out as a *township,* a paragraph which is in fact regularly employed in the Instructions to Governors, last appearing in those issued to Sir Thomas Brisbane in February 1821 (see p. 136 below).

Township was used in the United States from 1759,[9] from 1785 with the specific meaning of an area six miles square divided into thirty-six square miles called *sections,* an area which 'came to be a basic unit in the land system of the country'.[10] It is first recorded in Australian English in a letter from Governor Phillip to the Rt Hon. W. W. Grenville, dated 17 June 1790:

> The impossibility of conveying stores and provisions for any distance inland will oblige me to mark out the first

[9] Mathews, *Dictionary of Americanisms*: 'Any one of various tracts, differing in size, into which public land is surveyed'.

[10] J. T. Adams (ed.), *The Dictionary of American History*, p. 973.

township near Rose Hill, where there is a considerable
extent of good land. The sea-coast does not offer any
situation within our reach at present which is calculated
for a town whose inhabitants are to be employed in
agriculture.[11]

The meaning of *township*, as it is used here, is made
clearer in a paragraph relating to the laying out of townships, first used in the Instructions to Governor Hunter,
dated 23 June 1794:

> 19. And whereas it has been found by experience that
> the settling planters in townships hath very much re-
> dounded to their advantage, not only with respect to
> the assistance they have been able to afford each other in
> their civil concerns, but likewise with regard to their
> security, you are therefore to lay out townships of con-
> venient size and extent in such places as you in your
> discretion shall judge most proper, having, as far as may
> be, natural boundaries extending up into the country
> and comprehending a necessary part of the seacoast
> where it can conveniently be had.
> 20. You are also to cause a proper place in the most
> convenient part of each township to be marked out for
> the building of a town sufficient to contain such a
> number of families as you shall judge proper . . . and
> you are also to reserve to us proper quantities of land in
> each township for the following purposes, vizt.:—For
> erecting fortifications and barracks, or for other military
> or naval services, and more particularly for the building
> a town-hall and such other public edifices as you shall
> deem necessary, and also for the growth and production
> of naval timber, if there are woodlands fit for that
> purpose.[12]

That the word continued to be used in this sense for some
time is clear from the following quotations:

> I was directed to survey the Colony, and divide it into
> Counties, Townships, and Sections of a Square Mile,
> reserving in each Township four Square Miles or 2,560

[11] *H.R.A.*, vol. i, p. 182.
[12] Ibid., p. 526.

Acres in the most eligible situation for future Villages, etc., ...[13]

To confine them in this manner appears to me moreover to be in conformity with the agreement which they entered into on leaving England, which was that they should be settled on a Township of 110,000 acres, . . . A Township can, I apprehend, have no meaning other than a continuous block of land. . . .[14]

As early as 1811 Governor Macquarie used *township* as synonymous with *town* or *village*,[15] but the American use of the word to describe a unit of land measurement in surveying seems to have persisted beside this, its older English use, at least till 1840, with the result that a degree of confusion has developed over the word's meaning in the colony's first fifty years.

[13] Surveyor-General Oxley to Governor Darling, 26 January 1826, ibid., vol. xii, p. 380. In an earlier letter to Governor Macquarie (10 March 1817; ibid., vol. ix, p. 370) Oxley wrote: 'I respectfully beg to observe that I consider the Terms *Township* and *District* as Synonimous, although the latter has been commonly applied in all descriptions of Land granted here.'

[14] Sir George Gipps to Lord Russell, 6 October 1840; ibid., vol. xxi, p. 11. In an earlier letter to Russell (7 May 1840, ibid., vol. xx, p. 607) Gipps uses the word as a synonym for *village*: '. . . a New Township or Village, which is to be laid out at the distance of about nine miles from the residence of the Missionaries'.

[15] Governor Macquarie to the Earl of Liverpool, 8 October 1811 (ibid., vol. vii, p. 399, Enclosure): '. . . the Governor has deemed it expedient . . . to erect certain Townships on the most contiguous and eligible high Grounds . . . for the purpose of rendering every possible Accommodation and Security to the Settlers whose farms are exposed to the Floods . . . each Settler will be assigned an Allotment of Ground for a Dwelling-House, Offices, Garden, Corn-Yard and Stock-Yard proportioned to the extent of the Farm he holds within the influence of the Floods; but it is to be clearly understood that the Allotments so given, being intended as places of Security for the Produce of the Lands on the Banks of the Hawkesbury and Nepean . . . are to be always considered as forming an inseparable part of the said Farms' (of Windsor, Richmond, Pitt Town, Wilberforce, Castlereagh). Cf. Macquarie to Bathurst, 28 April 1814 and 8 June 1816 (ibid., vol. viii, p. 154 and vol. ix, pp. 140-1).

The *Oxford English Dictionary*, for instance, defines a specifically Australian use of *township* which reflects this confusion:

> In Australia. A site laid out prospectively for a town, meanwhile often consisting of a few 'shanties' grouped around a railway station, store, hotel, post office, or the like; a village or hamlet.[16]

It is probable that usages like the following, in which it is sometimes not clear which meaning was intended, account for this definition of *township*:

> We reached Gundiguy, at which the main rode to Port Phillip crosses that river and where a Township has been (recently) laid out, ...[17]

> We have had land presented in most of the neighbouring Townships and the inhabitants are pressing hard upon us to build places of Worship.[18]

> It is, of course, very plain, that Ipswich, now not only fixed upon by Government, but also surveyed and [*sic*] laid out as a township, is a place where a church of the living God is required; . . . .[19]

Section, used in the United States from 1785 for 'a portion of land one mile square (640 acres), forming 1/36 of a township',[20] occurs in Australian English with no change of meaning:

> . . . Mr. Chapman, who has intimated his selection of two Sections near me, has agreed . . . to Superintend my Farm and Stock, etc. . . .[21]

[16] See '*Township* 6'; see also H. W. King, 'County, Shire and Town in New South Wales', *Australian Geographer*, vol. vi (1954), no. 3, pp. 24-5.

[17] C. Sturt, Journal from May 22nd to June 20th, 1838.

[18] J. Eggleston to the Wesleyan Missionary Society, 5 September 1840.

[19] J. Gregor, Journal, 1843.

[20] Mathews, op. cit.

[21] A. M. Baxter to Col. Sec. Macleay, 23 May 1829, *H.R.A.*, vol. xiv, p. 781.

His Excellency Sir George Gipps at first gave sixteen sections of Land to be held in trust by the Society for the use of the Natives: but the Counsel being influenced it is supposed by some under current workers would not consent for us to have but one Section (which is Six hundred and forty Acres). . . .[22]

It may be essential however here to observe that wherever land is of a quality or in a locality, which renders it fit for cultivation, as in districts of superior fertility or in the neighbourhood of Towns, it is usually divided into much smaller lots than Sections of Square miles; such smaller divisions are called 'Cultivation allotments', the word Section being made use of only for grazing land, and they are made to vary from 20 to 320 acres.[23]

Block and *location* are both words used to describe tracts of land of no fixed size; *block* is not recorded by the *Oxford English Dictionary* and *location* is given as an Australian word first recorded in 1828. The three American senses of *block*, 'a tract of land', develop one from another, the earliest sense being extended and widened.[24] By 1815 the word was being used of a 'block of lots', a sense close to the original, and by 1829 it was used loosely of tracts of land varying in size.

Block is recorded in Australia in 1841 when it is used of 'allotments' of land for grazing purposes:

His Excellency further remarked that, according to the terms of the said Order, a Special Survey must be taken in 'One block, of which, the outer boundaries only will be surveyed, and the allotment will be subject to all conditions which may be established in the Colony respecting the proportion of front to depth, water-front-

[22] F. Tuckfield to Wesleyan Missionary Society, 29 January 1840.

[23] Sir George Gipps to Lord Russell, 19 December 1840, *H.R.A.*, vol. xi, p. 127.

[24] 'A connected or compact mass of houses or other buildings, in later use especially one mainly or wholly occupying the space bounded by four streets;' (1796), Mathews, *Dictionary of Americanisms*.

age, reserves for roads, and other conditions of a similar nature.[25]

I have known very bad blocks sold at 40s. per acre.[26]

Location is recorded in American use in 1809 as 'a modern term, for a tract of land, of which the limits are defined, and the property conveyed to a purchaser. The same thing was formerly called a *plantation*.'[27] The word is not noticed by Morris but is first recorded in Australian English in 1822:

Rode to the stock-locations of two more cisalpine settlers, ten miles to the westward, and back.[28]

I would propose that a Township be marked out both at Twofold Bay and in some eligible spot on the Coast, to which Mr Batman's party has proceeded. The Town Allotments and a portion of the adjoining Territory might then be declared open to location according to the existing Regulations. . . .[29]

These four words, *township*, *section*, *block*, and *location*, have specific meanings in American English; their history in Australian English shows these meanings gradually weakening as the words came into fairly general use or, as with *township*, the American meaning came into conflict with a better-established British usage. The remaining four words, *bush*, *bushranger*, *landshark*, and *squatter*, seem to have been borrowed in the same way but to have moved much more quickly into general currency.

Bush is widely used in the United States, Australia, New Zealand, and South Africa. Baker, whose earliest record of the word is dated 1803, traces it through South African

[25] Sir George Gipps to Lord Russell; Encl., 6 March 1841, *Minutes of the Proceedings of the Executive Council*, 26 February 1841; *H.R.A.*, vol. xxi, p. 265.

[26] *New South Wales, its Past, Present and Future Condition.*

[27] Mathews, *Dictionary of Americanisms.*

[28] Field, *Journal of an Excursion across the Blue Mountains*, p. 46.

[29] Sir Richard Bourke to Lord Glenelg, 10 October 1835, *H.R.A.*, vol. xviii, p. 157.

English to Dutch, but there is no evidence for this;[30] Morris, following the *Oxford English Dictionary*, describes it as a 'recent, and probably a direct adoption of the Dutch *bosch*, in colonies originally Dutch'. The word occurs early in the United States,[31] as does *bushranger*, and it is probable that both words were borrowed into Australian English from American. Governor Hunter uses *bush* in 1800 without commenting on it as a specifically Australian usage,[32] but later writers use it in a way which suggests no real familiarity with the word:

... woods, or bush, as it is called here. . . .[33]

'Bush' is the term commonly used for country *per se*: 'he resides in the Bush', implies that the person does not reside in, or very near, a town.[34]

Bushranger is first recorded in American English in 1758:

Outside of ordinary meal-times the following Brethren need butter: the night-watchman, the herdsmen, the Bush-Ranger sometimes, the threshers, and sometimes the carpenters.[35]

Used in the United States with the sense of 'frontiersman' or 'woodsman', the word is almost certainly a translation of the Dutch *boschloper*, 'woods runner'. The intermediate forms *bossloper* and *bushloper* were both in use before 1758.[36] Early Australian quotations suggest that the word

---

[30] *Australian Language*, p. 315; no source given. There are no early quotations for the word in Pettman's *Africanderisms*.

[31] Mathews, in his *Dictionary of Americanisms*, gives a quotation dated 1657 which is translated from Dutch. His earliest English quotation is dated 1779. Craigie and Hulbert record *bush* from 1827.

[32] Hunter to Portland, 2 January 1800, *H.R.A.*, vol. II, p. 419.

[33] Dawson, *The Present State of Australia*, p. 48.

[34] Lieut Breton, *Excursions in New South Wales, Western Australia, and Van Diemen's Land*, p. 46.

[35] Mathews, *Dictionary of Americanisms*. Mathews gives quotations illustrating the use of the word in 1758, 1830, 1885, and 1947. Craigie and Hulbert record *bushranger* from 1830.

[36] Mathews gives quotations for *bossloper* from 1687, 1690, and 1691, for *bushloper* from 1694 and 1752. Later quotations are historical.

was first used in Australia of men who lived in and were familiar with the bush and that the use of the word to describe a highwayman or robber was a later development. It is foreshadowed, for instance, in a sentence from Flinders's journal:

> This little bear-like quadruped is known in New South Wales, and called by the natives, *womat, wombat,* or *womback,* according to the different dialects, or perhaps to the different renderings of the wood rangers who brought the information. . . .[37]

The following quotations, which are the earliest Australian uses of the word I have found, possibly mark a transitional stage in the meaning of *bushranger*:

> If the Bush rangers will always bring plants from the remote parts of their tours, I can form a good idea of what distance they have been . . . If all the Bush rangers were to swear they had been at the Devils Wilderness, I would not believe them much more.[38]

> The whole of their Story is so contradictory that I should not have inserted these particulars but to prove what little Confidence can be put in this Class of what is locally termed Bush Rangers.[39]

But quotations given by Mathews for *bossloper* and *bushloper* suggest that these words may well have had a pejorative sense in the United States, something of which may have carried over into the Australian use of the word. At any rate, by 1820, as the following quotations indicate, *bushranger* was firmly established in Australia in the sense of highwayman:

> The principal part of the Shipping touching only at the Derwent, the Articles of Trade required at Port Dalrymple are consequently sent thither over Land. All which, together with the Herds, Flocks and Grain of the

[37] Journal, 1798, as quoted in Morris.
[38] G. Caley to Sir Joseph Banks, 19 July 1805, Banks Papers, vol. 20.
[39] Governor King to Lord Camden, 1 November 1805, *H.R.A.*, vol. v, p. 593.

Settlers, are now Subjected to the plunder of these Banditti, Commonly Called '*Bush Rangers*', Who in the present State of the Country are beyond All Control.[40]

From the Bushrangers to the Honor'ble T. Davey, Lieutenant Governor of Van damand's Land.[41]

. . . these men were united with a Banditti, who marauded about in the woods, and are designated in this Colony Bush Rangers, Men of the most alarming and dangerous description, who, lost to all sense of moral or social Duties, live by plundering the honest Settler of the Property he may have acquired by his Industry.[42]

Landshark is recorded by Mathews in the United States in 1829 and is used as a verb in 1841, in a letter from Sir George Gipps to Lord Russell:

. . . the practice, which in New South Wales is called 'Land Sharking,' is likely to flourish, and be improved upon, under the operation of a fixed price for Land in New Zealand.[43]

As a noun it is used by Howitt in 1853 in one of his vivid descriptions of the colony:

The most drunken population in the world!—a population refused land to live on, and preyed on by the most voracious land-sharks![44]

But an older English word, *landjobber*, recorded by the *Oxford English Dictionary* from 1745, seems to have been used, at least in the period before 1850, more commonly than *landshark*.

There is, finally, *squatter*. C. P. Hodgson, in 1846, described this as 'a word not to be met with in Johnson's

---

[40] Governor Macquarie to Earl Bathurst, 7 October 1814, ibid., vol. VIII, p. 307.

[41] Heading of a letter from M. Howe to Lieutenant Governor Davey 'written in blood' and dated 30 November 1816; T. E. Wells, *Michael Howe, The Last and Worst of the Bushrangers of Van Diemen's Land*.

[42] F. Garling to Governor Macquarie, 2 December 1817, *H.R.A.*, vol. IX, p. 513.

[43] Ibid., vol. XXI, p. 293.

[44] *Land, Labour and Gold*, vol. 2, p. 111.

Dictionary', one which, 'of Canadian extraction', meant 'literally to sit on the haunches' and was widely used of sheep-farmers in Australia 'from their being obliged frequently to adopt that position'.[45] It is of course formed from the verb, *to squat*, used in the United States in the sense of 'to settle on unclaimed land without a title'; and both the verb *to squat*, first recorded in Australian English in 1827, and the noun *squatter*, first recorded here in 1833, were borrowed from American English.

Squatter has moved through several stages in Australian English. Originally it was used with the same meaning as it had in the United States, and its connotations were invariably opprobrious:

... 'squatter' (the term is American) who are commonly, it may be said always, of the lowest grade.[46]

The Persons to whom Mr Burton alludes, familiarly called *Squatters*, are the object of great animosity on the part of the wealthier Settlers.[47]

A 'squatter' is a freed, or 'ticket-of-leave' man, who builds a hut with bark on unoccupied ground, buys or steals a few animals, sells spirits without a licence, receives stolen goods, and so at last becomes rich and turns farmer: he is the horror of all his honest neighbours.[48]

By 1840, however, the change in the squatters' circumstances described above by Darwin had taken place, and the word had come to mean 'one occupying a tract of pastoral land as tenant of the Crown'. Gipps uses *squatter* in this sense and describes the squatters as 'a class of persons whom it would be wrong to confound with those who bear the same name in America'.[49]

[45] *Reminiscences of Australia*, p. 4.

[46] Breton, *Excursions in New South Wales, Western Australia and Van Diemen's Land* (1833), p. 442.

[47] Sir Richard Bourke to Lord Glenelg, 18 December 1835, *H.R.A.*, vol. xviii, p. 230.

[48] C. R. Darwin, *Journey Across the Blue Mountains* (1836), p. 44.

[49] Sir George Gipps to Lord Russell, 19 December 1840, *H.R.A.*, vol. xxi, p. 130. For a full discussion of the word's history see S. H. Roberts, *The Squatting Age in Australia, 1835-1847*, pp. 66-84.

It is from this use of the word that the compounds *squat-tocratic* and *squattocracy* were formed and, once the word had come to be used to designate a class of people rather than a sort of tenancy, it was but a small step to extend and generalize the word's meaning, to use it loosely, as it is used now, of pastoralists with large freehold properties.

The second group of borrowings from American English, that made up of words from the American goldmining vocabulary, is a much more obvious and straightforward example of the borrowing process. The earliest words recorded are found in descriptions of the Californian gold-fields published here. Two of these, the earliest I have seen, are the anonymous *Digger's Handbook and Truth about California* and Wierzbicki's *Guide to the Gold Regions*,[50] both of which describe conditions on the gold-fields and the methods used to obtain alluvial gold. Both use a number of American words but neither is as useful from a lexicographical point of view as S. Rutter's *Hints to Gold Hunters*. Rutter's hints are based on his experiences in California (there is no evidence in the book of a first-hand knowledge of the Australian goldfields) and addressed to 'gold hunters' in Australia. The book demonstrates clearly the way in which mining techniques and the accompanying descriptive vocabulary were transferred from one country to another, a transference which is further illustrated by a passage in *Our Antipodes*, in which Mundy describes the reaction in Sydney in 1851 to the discovery of gold in Australia:

> Sydney assumed an entirely new aspect. The shop fronts put on quite new faces. Wares suited to the wants and tastes of general purchasers were thrust ignominiously out of sight, and articles of outfit for goldmining only were displayed. Blue and red serge shirts, Californian hats, leathern belts, 'real gold-digging gloves', mining-boots, blankets white and scarlet, became the show-goods in the fashionable streets. The pavements were lumbered with picks, pans and pots; and the gold-wash-ing machine, or Virginian 'cradle', hitherto a stranger

[50] Published as an appendix to E. Bryant's *What I Saw in California*.

in our eyes, became in two days a familiar household detail. . . . The newspapers teemed with advertisements pointing the same way: 'Waterproof tents for the El Dorado'—'Quicksilver for amalgamating gold-soil'—'Superfine biscuits packed in tins' . . . 'Cradles, prospecting pans, galvanised iron buckets, etc.' . . . 'Digger's Handbook, or Gold Digger's Guide, gratis to purchasers of outfit at ———— and ————'s stores.'[51]

There is an obvious American contribution to the equipment which Mundy notices, and the mention of a 'Digger's Handbook' gives some indication of the probable circulation of books of this sort.

We may assume, then, that the use of goldmining terms in these three books, and in others of their type, illustrates a transitional stage in which the words had a limited but growing currency in Australian English, although they had no Australian application. In later descriptions of the Australian goldfields these and many other words of American origin have become fully a part of the Australian vocabulary.

Sometimes these words are first used with an obvious awareness of their unfamiliarity to Australian readers. Thus Rutter qualifies his use of the word *bar*:

> . . . what in California they call a BAR, which we should call a sand bank, is formed in the middle of the river, or on its sides.[52]

And Mundy, similarly, explains his use of the word by coupling it with a known synonym in the phrase 'banks and bars'.[53] A less informed reaction is that of Lancelott who, describing likely places to prospect, in *Australia As It Is*, refers to 'a long sloping bend (called a bar by the Australian diggers)'.[54]

The compound *gold hunter*, although used without qualification or affectation by Rutter in the title of his book, is apologized for by Wierzbicki:

[51] Vol. 3, pp. 306-7.
[52] *Hints to Gold Hunters*, p. 9.
[53] *Our Antipodes*, vol. 3, p. 393.
[54] *Australia As It Is, Its Settlements, Farms and Gold Fields*, vol. 2, p. 22.

On arriving in California, the gold hunters, if we may be pardoned the expression, first touch the shore at San Francisco.[55]

Some of the words borrowed from California are not American coinages or new formations but words with a long history in British English which gained a fresh currency on the American goldfields. *Cradle*, for instance, is recorded in the *English Dialect Dictionary* as Northumbrian, but was almost certainly borrowed into Australian English from American. It is used by Bryant[56] and again by Rutter in his description of the Californian goldfields,[57] before being adopted fairly generally in Australia and used here both as a noun and a verb.

Digger, similarly, is an English word first recorded in the sixteenth century, but it became current in America in the early nineteenth century as one of several names given to prospectors. Thence it was brought to Australia and used at first with this general reference to 'all persons who searched for gold', later being 'generally restricted to those who seek for gold in the shallow alluviums'.[58] *Diggings* (along with the colloquial form *diggins*) followed the same course; as did *gold-washer*, for one who washes auriferous material to separate out the gold. *Dirt*, an old Norse word for 'excrement', borrowed into early Middle English either with this sense specifically or with more general reference to unclean matter or filth, developed in the seventeenth century an uncoloured reference to earth, mud, or soil, and, in the eighteenth century, the meaning it has for miners:

'Dirt' is the word universally used in California to signify the substance dug; earth, clay, gravel, or loose slate. The miners talk of rich dirt and poor dirt, and

[55] *Guide to the Gold Regions*, p. 144.

[56] *What I Saw in California*, p. 125; (the word occurs in a letter dated 1848).

[57] Op. cit., p. 12.

[58] R. B. Smyth, *The Goldfields and Mineral Districts of Victoria*, p. 609.

of stripping off so many feet of 'top dirt' before getting to the 'pay dirt'.[59]

Words like *digger* and *dirt* were part of the colloquial vocabulary of the miners. A number of compounds, *gold-digger, gold-diggings, gold district, gold fever* (also *yellow fever*), and *gold seeker,* were words of the same class, in vogue for the goldrush period but thereafter found only in historical contexts. One interesting and now probably obsolete expression is *to salt a claim,* meaning 'to sprinkle salt over the dirt', the salt having the appearance of gold-dust and giving the impression that the miner concerned has 'struck it rich'. Howitt uses *pepper* with the same meaning,[60] as does Thatcher in 'The Green New-Chum':

Of course you know they peppered it,
The gold was all a hum;
They'd sold it me because they saw
I was a green new-chum.[61]

Other words which, during their period of greatest currency, developed new and figurative uses are as much a part of the colloquial vocabulary now as they were then: the noun *claim,* for instance; *find,* in the sense of 'a good prospect'; *to jump,* as in 'to jump a claim'; *pile,* the dream of every miner 'buoyed up with the hope of some day being fortunate enough to drop on what was called in Colonial parlance "a pile" and so get rewarded for any past lost time';[62] and *rush* (as in *goldrush*).

More technical terms were also borrowed. Both on the Californian fields and in Australia the distinction was made between *wet diggings* and *dry diggings,* between 'those carried on in the bed of a river' and those worked on the banks or 'in the general spread of drift lying over

---

[59] Borthwick, *California,* p. 120 (as quoted in the *Oxford English Dictionary*).

[60] *Land, Labour and Gold,* vol. 1, p. 174.

[61] Stewart and Keesing (ed.), *Old Bush Songs,* p. 101.

[62] G. D. O'Byrne, Reminiscences of my Three Voyages to Australia and Sixteen Years Experience as a Gold Miner on the Principal Fields of Victoria (1889-91), vol. 3, p. 2.

the country'.[63] And the equipment used on the diggings included the *dipper*, the *pan* (the use of which gave rise to the derivative forms, *to pan off*, *to pan out*, and *to pan-wash*) and an outsize version of the cradle called the *Long Tom*.

Prospect, both as a noun and a verb, and *prospector* were also of American origin. *Prospect* was first used in the United States in the 1830s in the sense of 'a place where gold is likely to be found', and it came later to be used of 'the yield of gold from a dish of wash-dirt'.[64] These are both easily explained developments from the common British use of *prospect* for 'something to look forward to' or 'an expectation, or reason for looking forward to something'. Only the second of these seems to have been current in Australia. As a verb, meaning 'to search for gold or other minerals', *prospect* is found in the United States in the 1840s, and gives rise to the derivative noun, *prospector*. All forms were in general use in Australia by 1852, the *prospector* having already established himself as something more than an ordinary *gold seeker*. Thus we find Howitt, in his journal entry for February 1853, describing him as

> a peculiar character, worth noticing. He is a cautious mortal. He steals quietly away through the woods— generally, at first, taking a direction opposite to that which he means to follow. He is sometimes on foot, sometimes on horseback, carrying, besides his swag, a spade, a pick, and a tin-dish, to examine the soil of the creeks, or their banks.[65]

It is only to be expected that, along with occupational words of this sort, the miners should have brought words which related more generally to the conditions under which they lived on the goldfields and in the bush, and colloquial or slang words which were as much at home in the city as in the country. Most of these would have been

---

[63] J. B. Jukes (ed.), *Lectures on Gold for the Instruction of Emigrants about to Proceed to Australia*, p. 13.

[64] Mathews, *Dictionary of Americanisms*.

[65] *Land, Labour and Gold*, vol. 1, p. 208.

used more frequently in spoken English than in written, so their history, both in American use and Australian, is therefore much harder to document. The few words discussed here, most of which are recorded in Australian English between 1850 and 1880, should therefore most emphatically not be taken as a complete list but as an indication of the areas of the vocabulary in which, when a more extensive range of sources has been scanned, an important American influence may well be found.

Some of these words relate to makeshift equipment or techniques which miners and settlers used, words like *bowie knife, corduroy road, johnnycake,* and *splitrail fence.* A *bowie knife,* which Howitt for one repeatedly refers to as part of the Australian miner's regular attire, is a heavy sheath knife, more often than not fashioned out of an old file or piece of metal. First recorded in American English in 1836, it perpetuates the name of its maker, although it is frequently associated with his brother, one of the heroes of the Alamo.[66] *Corduroy road,* in United States and Canadian use in the 1820s and 1830s, describes the use of half-trees in bridging swampy patches on a road:

> In loose and swampy parts they saw trees in two, from the top to the roots, and then place the flat-side of the half trees upon the ground, and the coach rattles and jolts over the round upper half of the trees. Roads thus formed are called 'corduroy', from their striped resemblance to that material.[67]

Bowie knife and *corduroy road* seem to have acquired a fairly limited currency in the 1850s and 1860s, unlike *splitrail fence,* which was in fairly general use by the end of the century, and *johnnycake,* which has taken its place along with other delicacies of bush cooking: G. F. Angas, in 1850, refers to a banquet of *dampers, doughboys, leatherjackets, johnnycakes,* and *beggars-in-the-pan,*[68] all variations on a theme of flour and water, with which his cook once confronted him.

---

[66] Mathews, *Dictionary of Americanisms.*

[67] F. J. Jobson, *Australia,* p. 99.

[68] *Savage Life and Scenes in Australia and New Zealand,* vol. 1, p. 161.

Obviously of goldfields origin is the use of *John* or *John Chinaman* for a Chinese, and there are several other slang words related to the amusements miners and settlers found for themselves: *ante* 'the preliminary stake in a game like poker', along with the phrase, *to ante up*; *monte*, in American English the name of a game of chance, in Australian a synonym for 'certainty'; *runner*, or 'in common parlance, a tout for a hotel';[69] and *shanty*. *Shanty*, derived either from Canadian-French *chantier*, 'a log hut', or Irish *sean-tig*, 'an old, miserable hut', was in use in the United States from the 1820s: in Australia it has been used, at least from the 1860s, with the sense of either 'a mean, tumbledown shack' or 'a sly grog shop in the bush'.

These two small groups of colloquial words, the one associated with the equipment and techniques of the settlers and the other with their amusements, come as inevitable adjuncts to the occupational vocabulary of the miners, and serve to indicate a possible American source for words borrowed into a part of the Australian vocabulary which, in the latter half of the nineteenth century, was expanded rapidly in size and currency.

---

[69] O'Byrne, Reminiscences (1889-91), vol. 3, p. 6.

L

8

Borrowings from the Languages of Immigrant Minorities

THE VOCABULARY of American English has been greatly enriched with borrowings from the languages of other European settlers. French, Spanish, Dutch, and German words are not uncommon and the character of the borrowings in each case reflects the nature of the contact between the two peoples. Thus, from Spanish are borrowed words to do with ranch life, such as *buckaroo, corral, lariat, lasso, ranch, rodeo,* and *stampede,* from German a great number of words for food and drink, such as *delicatessen, hamburger, lager beer, sauerkraut,* and *schnitzel* (all of which have subsequently been borrowed into other branches of English).

In Australia the historical situation is different. There were no other European colonies, such as the French, Spanish, and Dutch in America; nor have any later immigrant groups made any impact on Australian culture comparable with that of the Germans, Italians, and Jews in America. Chinese, Germans, and Italians have each settled in immigrant pockets for periods of a generation or more, but in none of these instances have relations between the immigrant minorities and the Australians been of the sort that would facilitate linguistic exchange.

Alien communities have either dissipated rapidly, as did the Scandinavian (see p. 158 below), or retained their own cultural and linguistic identity, as did the Italian (for the first generation at least), German, and Chinese. Settlements have been small and isolated, and external contacts have been desultory, unlikely to have any significant influence on an unreceptive Australian majority.

At no time has the non-British element of the population been large: only 7·2 per cent of the total in 1861, 5 per cent in 1891, and 2 per cent in 1947. Of the 83,395 non-Britishers in Australia in 1861 nearly half (39,000) were Chinese labourers, many of whom came to the goldfields under contract to Chinese merchants and, on the goldfields, 'camped together, aloof and apart from the other diggers'.[1] By 1891, as a result of the restrictive policies adopted by the colonies, the Chinese made up only 22 per cent of the non-British population, a percentage which continued to drop as a result of the Commonwealth restriction on Chinese immigration in 1901. The Chinese miners were numerous, industrious, and frugal: the early opposition of the Europeans, allied with the tendency of the Chinese to keep together and apart from the other settlers, kept the day-to-day contact of Australians with Chinese to a minimum. Chinese settlement on the goldfields, like that of the Kanakas in Queensland in the 1890s,[2] was of economic rather than socio-cultural importance, so the probability of anything other than occasional slang words being borrowed was small.

At first sight German settlement in South Australia and later in Queensland would seem likely to lead to linguistic borrowing. The German settlers were highly regarded by the British, they came as permanent settlers, were independent and socially the equals of the British and, at least

---

[1] N. P. O. Pyke, 'Some Leading Aspects of Foreign Immigration to the Goldfields', *Royal Australian Historical Society Journal and Proceedings*, vol. 33, pt 1 (1947), p. 7. Cf. C. Daley, 'The Chinese in Victoria', *Victorian Historical Magazine*, vol. 14 (1929), p. 29, 'On the goldfields the Chinese, unlike other immigrants, did not merge with other diggers, but, perforce, kept themselves in separate camps, herding in narrow streets in calico tents or huts of bark and saplings . . .' See also G. Serle, *The Golden Age*.

[2] See G. C. Bolton, *A Thousand Miles Away*. There is a brief account of Kanaka immigration in J. Lyng's *Non-Britishers in Australia*; also of a similar, smaller labour force of Afghans in Central Australia. Afghans were first brought to Australia as camel drivers about 1860 and never numbered more than 400 (1901). An interesting survival is *Ghan Town* along with the fairly common abbreviation *Ghan*.

until World War I, made up a significant proportion of the population in the parts of South Australia and Queensland where their settlements were closest. Borrie estimates that in the latter half of the nineteenth century almost one-tenth of the population of South Australia were of German descent, living mainly in group settlements inland from Adelaide.[3]

One would have expected that as communications were improved, cities built, and these settlements drawn into close contact with the Australians about them, the initial isolated settlements would disintegrate, external contacts exerting a stronger pull on the settlers than the retention of language, customs, and religion in the home and church. That this did not happen was due to the influence of the Lutheran Church, whose pastors were largely German-born and almost entirely German-trained,[4] to the existence of a German language press and German-speaking schools, clubs, and societies which maintained an active interest in the culture of the Fatherland.

Hebart, describing the strength of this *Deutschtum* in the years before World War I, writes:

> Everywhere, even in the more isolated parishes of the South Australian North, the German language and customs held absolute sway in the home and in the church. So tenaciously and jealously did they cling to this heritage that they looked askance at a pastor if he should now and then use 'English scraps'. They looked

[3] W. D. Borrie, *Italians and Germans in Australia: A Study of Assimilation*, p. 161.

[4] C. A. Price, *German Settlers in South Australia*, p. 19, writes that the Lutheran Church sought to maintain *Deutschtum* in Australia 'to keep faith pure and free from the influence of other denominations. But such belief, according to some recent Lutheran writers, involves no more than that the leaders of the Lutheran churches abroad should keep in close contact with church doctrine and developments in Germany or America or wherever they arise; it does not necessarily mean that all Lutherans abroad should maintain their Deutschtum, speak the German language, preserve the German culture and customs. Yet this is how the nineteenth century churchmen in Australia interpreted their belief. In so doing it is clear that they were deeply influenced by the pan-Germanic ideals spreading throughout German circles the whole world over.'

upon him as the official guardian of Deutschtum. . . .
How much could one praise the steady tenacity of this
generation, the fact that German folk-songs and folk-
hymns lived among these German people in their homes.
The large and the small Missionsharfs, Pilgerharfs,
Dolker and old collections were in general use and
young people, visiting each other on Sunday afternoons,
cheerily sang the German lays.[5]

Similarly, in a short description of Hahndorf in 1908,
Hans Heysen notes that

. . . even now, after a lapse of more than half a century,
Hahndorf retains for the most part the characteristics of
a German village. The people speak their native tongue
and the primitive methods of agriculture are still in
vogue. One sees the good 'frau' in the fields working like
a man. . . .[6]

Bilingualism does not seem to have been common.
Within the settlements German was the 'prestige' language
and it is unlikely that an English-German mixture would
have been used for more than desultory conversation.

For quite different reasons from those affecting the
Chinese settlement the German communities in Australia
retained their identity from their foundation in 1838 into
the twentieth century, when Anglo-German rivalry overseas led to a temporary hardening of Australian attitudes
towards the German settlers and began a progressive
weakening of *Deutschtum*. The ban on the use of the
German language during World War I may well have
acted against the absorption of German words into Australian at a time when increasing contact between the two
groups might reasonably be expected to have led to some
borrowings. The effect of this reaction is most dramatically
illustrated by A. Lodewyckx, who lists the following
German place-names which were replaced by English
names at the time of World War I:

[5] T. Hebart, *Die Vereinigte Evangelische Lutherische Kirche in Australien*, p. 469.

[6] 'A German-Australian Viilage', *Lone Hand*, July 1908, p. 194.

New South Wales
 Germantown (Holbrook), German's Hill (Lidster), German Creek (Empire Vale)

Victoria
 Germantown (Grovedale), Hochkirch (Tarrington), Mount Bismarck (Mount Kitchener)

Queensland
 Bergen (Murra Murra), Bergenside (Neuve), Bismarck (Maclagan), Engelsburg (Kalbar), Gehrkevale (Mount Mort), Gramzow (Carbrook), Hapsburg (Kowbi), Hessenburg (Ingoldsby), Kirchheim (Haigslea), Murden (Frenchton), Roessler (Applethorpe), Stegeht (Woongoolba), Teutelburg (Willa), Fahley (Kilbirnie)

South Australia
 Bartsch's Creek (Yedlakoo Creek), Hundred of Basedow (Hundred of French), Cape Bauer (Cape Wondoma), Berlin Rock (Panpandie Rock), Bethanien (Bethany), Bismarck (Weeroopa), Blumberg (Birdwood), Blumental (Lakkari), Buchfelde (Loos), Carlsruhe (Kunden), Ehrenbreitstein (Mount Yerila), Ferdinand Creek (Ernaballa Creek), Mount Ferdinand (Mount Warrabillinna), Friedrichstadt (Tangari), Friedrichswalde (Tarnuma), Gebhardt's Hills (Polygon Ridge), German Creek (Benara Creek), German Pass (Tappa Pass), Germantown Hill (Vimy Ridge), Gottlieb's Well (Parnggi Well), Grünberg (Karalta), Grüntal (Verdun), Hahndorf (Ambleside), Hasse's Mound (Larelar Mound), Heidelberg (Kobandilla), Herrgott Springs (Marree), Hildesheim (Punthari), Hoffnungstal (Karrawirra), Hundred of Homburg (Hundred of Haig), Jaenschtown (Kerkanya), Kaiserstuhl (Mount Kitchener), Klaebes (Kilto), Klemzig (Gaza), Krause Rock (Marti Rock), Hundred of Krichauff (Hundred of Beatty), Krichauff (Beatty), Kronsdorf (Kabminye), Langdorf (Kaldukee), Langmeil (Bilyara), Lobetal (Tweedvale), Mount Meyer (Mount Kauto), Müller's Hill (Yandina Hill), Neudorf (Mamburdi), Neukirch (Dimchurch), New Hamburg (Willyaroo), New Mecklenburg (Gomersal), Olivental (Olivedale), Hundred of Paech (Hundred of Cannawigara), Petersburg (Peterborough), Hundred of Pflaum (Hundred

of Geegeeia), Rhine Park (Kongolia), Rhine Hill (Mons), Rhine River North (The Somme), Rhine River South (The Marne), Rhine Villa (Cambrai), Hundred of Rhine North (Hundred of Jellicoe), Hundred of Rhine South (Hundred of Jutland), Rosental (Rosedale), Hundred of Scherk (Hundred of Sturdee), Schöntal (Boongala), Hundred of Schomburgke (Hundred of Maude), Seppelts (Dorrien), Schreiberhau (Warre), Siegersdorf (Bultawilta), Steinfeld (Stonefield), Summerfeldt (Summerfield), Vogelsang's Corner (Teerkoore), Hundred of von Doussa (Hundred of Allenby), Wusser's Nob (Karun Nob)

Western Australia
   Muller Park (Kitchener Park)

Tasmania
   Bismarck (Collins Vale).[7]

The list provides a fascinating demonstration of some of the ways in which place-names are chosen.

Since 1891 the most important immigrant minority has been Italian, the numbers of Italian-born immigrants rising from almost 4,000 in 1891 to almost 228,000 in 1961. This does not seem a significant proportion of the population until it is realized that, like the Germans, the Italians have tended to settle in pockets, partly because of the narrow range of occupations in which they were engaged and partly because the first-generation settlers in an area frequently attracted out members of their family or of their rural community in Italy. Yet Italian group settlements were never as isolated as the German: first-generation Italians, preoccupied with establishing themselves materially in a new country, generally continued to speak Italian but their children learnt English at school and at play and became to some extent bilingual.[8] The Australian worker showed some antagonism towards the Italian, largely because of his willingness to work 'from dawn to dusk, Saturdays and Sundays included, whereas

---

[7] *Die Deutschen in Australien*, p. 252.

[8] Borrie, *Italians and Germans*, and C. Gamba, *The Italian Fishermen of Fremantle*, describe this pattern in Queensland and Fremantle respectively.

the award stipulated an eight-hour day, Sundays excluded',[9] but more important than this in reducing the possibility of lexical borrowing from Italian has been the Italians' adoption of the living habits and occupational techniques of their Australian neighbours. Their group settlements have not been 'closed' in the sense that the group settlements of Germans in South Australia and Queensland were, and there has been no attempt to form 'little Italies' or to retain features of Italian culture and life which might lead to additions to the Australian English vocabulary.[10]

Scandinavian immigration to Australia reached a peak in 1891 when there were 16,500 Danes, Norwegians, and Swedes in Australia, most of them in Queensland. But these have been readily absorbed into the Australian community, the scattered nature of their settlement, the diversity of their occupations, and their high degree of intermarriage with Australians acting against the growth of group settlements.[11] A few place-names survive as testimony to the presence of Scandinavians in Australia, but none of these is necessarily indicative of the extent of Scandinavian settlement and some may well have come through British English:

New South Wales
   Bredbo, Greenland, Norway, Uppsall's Creek

Victoria
   Alexandra, Greenland Dam, Fryerstown, Peterson, Walhalla, Moe

Queensland
   Archer, Biskdale, Eidsvold, Lower Tivoli, Marmor, Point Archer

South Australia
   Lyrup

[9] Borrie, *Italians and Germans*, p. 110.

[10] The assimilation of Greeks, on a smaller scale, has largely followed the Italian pattern: see C. A. Price, *Southern Europeans in Australia*.

[11] See W. D. Borrie, 'Australia', in O. Handlin and B. Thomas (ed.), *The Positive Contribution by Immigrants*, p. 95.

Western Australia
  Bornholm, Bowgade, Denmark, Norseman

Tasmania
  Drik Drik.[12]

Of the important minorities, Chinese, German, Italian, and Scandinavian, none has added significantly to the Australian cultural pattern or, incidentally, to Australian English, partly because the settlers either attempted to exclude the Australian majority, as did the Germans and Chinese, or became absorbed in it as did the Scandinavians and Italians, and partly because Australians have been unreceptive, often hostile, to any way of living other than their own. The general character of these relationships suggests, *a priori*, that linguistic borrowings would be made from Australian rather than into it, and this is borne out by evidence from South Australian German, the one minority language in Australia which has been properly examined.

Lodewyckx lists a number of English borrowings into South Australian German which he has recorded from the German language press. Almost all of these are translations of English or Australian words and were pronounced, Lodewyckx adds, as nearly to the English as possible. The most interesting of these are the borrowings from Australian: *viehstation*, 'cattle station', *schafstation*, 'sheep station', *bundlemann*, 'swagman', *herdenmann*, 'stockman', *land aufnehmen*, 'to take up land', *kricke*, 'creek', and *ich buddelete oben in Kimberley*, 'I buddled'. There are also a number of transliterations of commonly used English words and colloquial phrases: *tanz*, 'dance', *stab*, 'staff', *partie*, 'party', *fluten*, 'floods', *gebrochen*, 'broke' (financially), *uberkommen*, 'to overcome', *schnecken*, 'snakes', *manidschen*, 'to manage', *arrehndscht*, 'arranged', *kits*, 'kids', 'children', *land klaren*, 'to clear land', *aufringen*, 'to ring up', *geben Sie mir einen Ring*, 'please give me a ring' (on the telephone), *er hatist nicht aufgedreht*, 'he has

[12] J. Lyng, *The Scandinavians in Australia, New Zealand and the Western Pacific*, p. 104.

not turned up', *das kann ich nicht erfordern*, 'I cannot afford it'.[13]

There are few words of non-British origin in Australian English and little to suggest that these were borrowed first from the immigrant minorities: no words of Italian, Scandinavian, or Chinese origin are recorded, and the few German words listed by Morris, Baker, and Mitchell, *cronk, sane, shicer, slanter, spieler, spruiker*, and *swatser*,[14] seem almost certainly to have come into Australian English through English or American slang.

Morris first records *shicer*, used of an unproductive gold-mine, in 1861 and Mitchell, following Morris, gives *shicer*, 'a swindler', as a secondary usage developing from the goldmining term. The word is derived ultimately from German *scheissen*, as is the American *shyster*, first recorded in 1846 by Mathews, as 'a term of contempt for an un-scrupulous, tricky, mean person, often applied to lawyers'.[15] Mencken notes 'that the suffix *-ster* is not uncommon in English and that it usually carries a deprecatory signific-ance',[16] and it seems probable that this word and the Australian *shicer* are derived in the first instance from English slang. Hotten's comments are interesting and indicate that a form of the word had been used in Eng-land since 1796:

> *Shice*, nothing; 'to do anything for shice', to get no pay-

---

[13] Lodewyckx, op. cit., pp. 175-7.

[14] Morris and Baker derive *cronk* from German *krank*, 'sick' or 'ill'. The word is English slang, as A. G. Mitchell indicates, and is recorded by Grose in his *Classical Dictionary of the Vulgar Tongue* (1796), as *crank* 'a cant term for "the falling sickness" '.

Baker records *sane* (G. *zehn*, 'ten') and *swatser* (G. *schwarzer*, 'black'), the latter used of an Aboriginal. There is no recorded evidence of the use of either word in Australian English. A number of German words are used in Melanesian pidgin and it is possible that *swatser* is one of these.

Spruik and *spruiker* appear to be of Dutch rather than German derivation and may possibly be traced to the Cape settlement. They are not recorded in Pettman's *Africanderisms*, and are given by Webster's as Australian.

[15] *A Dictionary of Americanisms*.

[16] *The American Language* (4th ed.), p. 158.

ment. The term was first used by the Jews in the last
century. Grose gives the phrase *Chice-am-a-trice*, which
has a synonymous meaning. Spanish, *chico*, little; Anglo-
Saxon, *chiche*, niggardly.

Shicer, a mean man, a humbug, a 'duffer',—a person
who is either worthless or will not work.[17]

The use of *duffer* as a synonym for *shicer*, both in
eighteenth-century English meaning 'a worthless person'
and in Australian usage meaning 'an unproductive gold-
mine', supports this development.

Slanter (also *slinter*) is recorded by Baker as underworld
slang and derived from the Dutch *slenter*, 'a trick'. This is
probably correct, as *schlenter* is recorded in South African
English in the 1890s in the sense of 'dubious', 'untrust-
worthy', 'counterfeit'.[18] Downing records *slanter* or *schlanter*, 'a trick', also used in the phrase *to run a schlanter*, 'to
make no genuine effort to win a game'.[19]

Spieler (German *spielen*, 'to play') has been used in
American and Australian slang since the 1890s, in American for 'an actor or player, a voluble talker, as a "barker"
stationed outside an amusement place to attract custom-
ers',[20] and in Australian either in this sense or to describe a
'professional fraud, a cardsharper'.[21] In Mathews's earliest
quotation (1891) the word is used of a gambling 'operator',
and Hotten's recording of *spellken*, *speelken*, or *spielken*,
'a playhouse', suggests that the words have a common
origin in English slang and have developed independently.

Some unrecorded borrowings from German may be in
local use in parts of South Australia. Price noted that
streuselkuchen, 'cake', *mettwurst*, 'sausage', *nudelsuppe*,

---

[17] *A Dictionary of Modern Slang, Cant and Vulgar Words* (2nd
ed.).

[18] Pettman, *Africanderisms*. N. van Blerk, in a letter dated 27
April 1961, quotes N. Sabbagha: '*schlenter* seems to be a South
Africanism, which probably entered Australia through the English
of those Australians who sought their fortunes on the South African
diamond and gold fields in the late nineteenth century'.

[19] *Digger Dialects.*

[20] M. M. Mathews, op. cit.

[21] A. G. Mitchell, *Supplement . . . to Chambers's Shorter English
Dictionary*.

'macaroni soup', and *sauerkraut* had 'penetrated to the English colonists',[22] presumably independently of their use in British English. The South Australian word *butcher*, 'a glass of beer', is probably of German origin. Morris derives it from workers in a South Australian 'butchery who used this refreshment regularly', O'Brien and Stephens from German *becher*, 'a beaker or kind of lidded drinking jug'. O'Brien and Stephens note that the word was first used in Adelaide and is 'gradually spreading'.[23]

Clinah, 'girl', is recorded by Baker as German. The word was current in the 1890s and may well have come into Australian slang from South Australian German, as the following quotations suggest:

> And his ladylove's his 'donah',
> Or his 'clinah' or his 'tart',
> Or his 'little bit of muslin',
> As it used to be his 'bart'.[24]

The 'clinah' of Goodge's 'Australian Slanguage' is simply the German *Kleine* (female of *klein*, small, little, and meaning 'little', i.e., woman) Australised. I heard the term first in South Australia (where Germans abound) some years ago. 'Meine kleine' is the German youth's equivalent for 'my donah', or 'piece' or 'bart'.[25]

It seems unlikely that the growing numbers of immigrants this century will lead to Australian English borrowing more heavily than it did in the nineteenth.[26] Programmes for the teaching of English to New Australians have probably resulted in a greater degree of bilingualism amongst first-generation immigrants, but the emphasis on

[22] *German Settlers in South Australia*, p. 13.

[23] S. E. O'Brien and A. G. Stephens, Material for a Dictionary of Australian Slang (1910).

[24] From W. T. Goodge, *The Great Australian Slanguage* (1897), quoted in Baker, *The Australian Language*, p. 117.

[25] *Bulletin*, 20 August 1898.

[26] Baker, in *Australia Speaks*, pp. 222-30, suggests that New Australians may well 'have a sizeable influence over the years'. His only evidence, a few Hungarian translations of English words and a few examples of misused English words, is hardly a basis for this claim.

assimilation, or 'Australianizing', has offset this. The proportion of immigrants in the total population remains small and no one national group has had the opportunity of establishing itself, as the German settlers did in South Australia, as a separate 'colony', marked by its retention of the native language, institutions, and customs.

9

Conclusion

THE EVIDENCE presented in the preceding chapters argues for a conception of the Australian vocabulary different from that which is now widely held. It is true that the number of words discussed is not large and that, in each category, there were undoubtedly many more which came into general currency during the nineteenth century. And there is sufficient evidence to suggest what one would in any case expect, that a record of some local and occupational vocabularies would extend the lists still further. But it is the categories that are important: based on a fairly wide range of nineteenth-century sources and an assessment of the other records of the Australian vocabulary, they argue against the thesis that Australian English is an unusual linguistic phenomenon, and in favour of its being regarded as a natural extension of the British English vocabulary, occasioned by the new environment, fed by the existing vocabularies of the settlers, and controlled by their continued close ties with the mother country.

The two most important categories in the nineteenth century are the survivals and innovations in the language of the settlers (see chapters 4 and 5). These illustrate, on the one hand, a retention of existing vocabularies which were not part of Standard English and, on the other, both the extension of the meanings of many Standard English words and the formation, by the processes of composition or derivation from existing Standard English elements, of many more.

The retention of existing slang and regional dialect vocabularies is significant. During the nineteenth century many words from these vocabularies moved into general currency in British English, but those recorded as Australian are words which have either not become current in British English or which have become current in British English only after continued use in Australia. They are a mixed bag, mostly words of a fairly general character, relating to people, their activities and amusements. Most are colloquial and it is likely that a dialect survey would show many more words of this sort current in speech than have found their way into written documents. But, in a country where the agricultural and pastoral industries have been of the greatest economic and social importance, the number of words in general currency which relate to agriculture and animal husbandry is surprisingly small. The fact that, in the years before 1850 when the vocabulary was in its formative stages, most of the settlers and convicts were townspeople has clearly had its effect on the composition of the vocabulary. There has been a loss in the traditional vocabularies associated with rural pursuits and a corresponding gain in the use of a number of basic words which have become generalized in meaning and have been employed, along with a particularizing noun or adjective, in a variety of compounds.

This sort of expansion, where the usefulness of a vocabulary is increased as existing words develop new meanings or functions, is natural and straightforward: if *stock* is current for sheep and cattle and there are no traditionally used words for the people, actions and equipment involved in the handling of stock, the gap is most readily filled by the formation of such compounds as *stockman, stockwhip,* and *stockyard,* or by the transference of words such as *muster* from not altogether dissimilar contexts. It is wrong, particularly as most of the Australian compounds are straightforward and descriptive and show none of the love of word-play which is so pervasive in American English, to take words of this sort—and there are many more than are listed here—as evidence of the Australian's inventiveness. It would be nearer the truth to argue that the Australian has 'made do', improvised, accepted the materials nearest to hand and built up an essentially makeshift vocabulary—though this is not peculiarly Australian, as examples from any other branch of English at any period of its history would show.

Borrowings into Australian English, during the nineteenth century at any rate, are not so extensive or so pervasive in their use as to alter significantly the character of the vocabulary. Apart from a relatively small number of words used in Aboriginal pidgin, the borrowings from Aboriginal languages were all either the names of flora and fauna or words associated with the Aborigines' way of life which have remained in use only in this very restricted context. Those from American English belong to a small early group—more an historical curiosity than anything else—or to the vocabulary of mining, where they join a group of traditional dialect terms brought by British miners. In the second half of the century a growing number of colloquial Americanisms are found, but these do not reach significant proportions until they are reinforced by the first waves of twentieth-century American influence. The other immigrant minorities contributed little or nothing, and the only other branch of English with which one might have expected some interchange, New Zealand English, seems to have borrowed heavily from Australian but given little in return.

The impression that remains then, is of a vocabulary which reflects faithfully the origins and interests of the Australian people. It should not be vilified, as it was by English visitors who saw it as a barbarous corruption of the language their grammarians had done so much to refine; nor, on the other hand, should it be taken, as it sometimes has been by the over-patriotic, as a sign of the independence and vigour with which Australians have laid the foundations of a new nation.

Selected Bibliography

A. W. G. 'Australianisms and Their Origin', *Lone Hand*, November 1908.

Ackroyd, J. 'Lingo-Jingo', *Southerly*, no. 2, 1946.

Acland, L. G. D. 'Sheep Station Glossary' (1933) in *Early Canterbury Runs* (ed. A. Wall). Christchurch, N.Z., 1951.

Adams, J. T. *The Dictionary of American History*. New York, 1940.

Angas, G. F. *Savage Life and Scenes in Australia and New Zealand*. 2 vols. London, 1850.

'Anonymous Account of a Journey to the Blue Mountains', *H.R.N.S.W.*, vol. III.

'Aussies' Own Talk', *New York Times Magazine*, 22 March 1942.

Australian Comic Dictionary of Words and Phrases by 'Turner O. Lingo' (M. E. Fullerton). Sydney, 1916.

Australian Encyclopaedia. Sydney, 1958.

'Australia Needs More Slang', *Daily Telegraph* (Sydney), 14 July 1936.

'Australian Colloquialisms', *All the Year Round* (London), 30 July 1887.

Backhouse, James. *A Narrative of a Visit to the Australian Colonies*. London, 1843.

———— Report on the State of the Settlement of The Van Diemen's Land Company, 1833. MS. Society of Friends Library, London.

Baker, Sidney J. *A Popular Dictionary of Australian Slang*. Sydney, 1941.

———— *Australian Pronunciation*. Sydney, 1947.

———— 'Australian Rhyming Argot in the American Underworld', *American Speech*, vol. 19, 1944.

———— 'Australian Slang', *Australian Encyclopaedia*.

———— 'Australian Slang', *Encyclopaedia Britannica*, 1950 ed.

167

M

———— *Australia Speaks.* Sydney, 1953.

———— Dictionary of Australian Flora and Fauna. 1950. Typescript, Mitchell Library.

———— 'Home-Grown Idiom Goes to Work', *Sydney Morning Herald*, 18 October 1952.

———— 'Language', in A. L. McLeod, *The Pattern of Australian Culture.* Ithaca, N.Y., 1964.

———— 'Language and Character', in T. G. Hungerford (ed.), *Australian Signpost: An Anthology.* Melbourne, 1956. Also reprinted in *The Drum.*

———— *The Australian Language.* Sydney, 1945.

———— *The Drum.* Sydney, 1959.

———— 'The Influence of American Slang on Australian', *American Speech*, vol. 18, 1943.

———— 'The Literature of Pidgin English', *American Speech*, vol. 19, 1944.

———— 'Pidgin English', *Australian Encyclopaedia.*

———— 'Pidgin English', *Encyclopaedia Britannica*, 1950 ed.

Banister, T., and Mossman, S. *Australia Visited and Revisited.* London, 1853.

Banks Papers. Correspondence and Papers of Sir Joseph Banks, 1766-1822. 22 vols. Mitchell Library.

Barrallier, F. 'Barrallier's Journal', *H.R.N.S.W.*, vol. v, Appendix A.

Baugh, A. C. *A History of the English Language.* London, 1951.

Beaglehole, J. C. *The Endeavour Journal of Joseph Banks, 1768-1771.* 2 vols. Sydney, 1962.

Bevan, I. (ed.). *The Sunburnt Country.* London, 1953.

Bigge, J. T. *Report on the Commission of Inquiry into the State of the Colony of New South Wales.* London, 1822.

Blackburn, D. Papers. Mitchell Library.

Boldrewood, Rolf (T. A. Browne). *Robbery Under Arms.* London, 1898.

Bolton, G. C. *A Thousand Miles Away.* Brisbane, 1963.

Borrie, W. D. *Italians and Germans in Australia: A Study of Assimilation.* Melbourne, 1954.

—— 'Australia', in O. Handlin and B. Thomas (ed.). *The Positive Contribution by Immigrants*. Paris, 1955.

Bradish, C. R. 'The Australian Vernacular', *American Mercury*, July 1954.

Breton, —. *Excursions in New South Wales, Western Australia and Van Diemen's Land*. London, 1833.

Bride, T. F. *Letters from Victorian Pioneers: being a series of Papers on the early Occupation of the Colony, The Aborigines etc*. Melbourne, 1898.

Britton, J. H. An Investigation into the Source Materials of Australian Additions to the English Language. M.A. thesis, University of Sydney, 1938.

Brook, G. L. *English Dialects*. London, 1963.

Browne, T. A., *see* Boldrewood.

Bryant, E. *What I Saw in California*. Launceston, 1850.

Byrne, J. C. *Twelve Years' Wandering in the British Colonies*. 2 vols. London, 1848.

Capper, J. *Our Gold Colonies*. London, 1854.

Cecil, R. *Gold Fields Diary, 1852* (ed. E. Scott). Melbourne, 1935.

Chisholm, A. H. *The Making of a Sentimental Bloke*. Melbourne, 1946.

Churchward, L. G. 'The American Contribution to the Victorian Gold Rush', *Victorian Historical Magazine*, vol. 19, 1941-2.

Clark, C. M. H. *A Short History of Australia*. New York, 1963.

—— 'The Origins of the Convicts Transported to Eastern Australia, 1788-1852', *Historical Studies, Australia and New Zealand*, 1956, vol. 7, 1956, nos. 26 and 27.

Collins, D. *An Account of the English Colony in New South Wales* London, 1798; (ed. J. Collier). Christchurch, N.Z., 1910.

'Cooee, This is fair dinkum', *Rotarian*, June 1946.

Cotton, J. *Correspondence 1842-1849* (ed. G. Mackaness). Australian Historical Monographs series. Sydney, 1953.

Craigie, W. A., and Hulbert, J. R. *A Dictionary of American English on Historical Principles*. Chicago, 1938.

Crowe, Cornelius. *Australian Slang Dictionary*. Melbourne, 1895.

Cunningham, A. Tour into the Interior of New South Wales. Sturt Collection, Rhodes House, Oxford.

Cunningham, P. *Two Years in New South Wales*. 2nd ed. 2 vols. London, 1827.

Curr, E. M. *The Australian Race*. Melbourne, 1886.

D. L., *see Digger's Handbook and Truth about California*.

Dakin, W. J. *Whalemen Adventurers*. Sydney, 1933.

Daley, C. 'The Chinese in Victoria', *Victorian Historical Magazine*, vol. 14, 1929.

Darwin, C. R. *Journey across the Blue Mountains*, 1836 (ed. G. Mackaness). Australian Historical Monographs series. Sydney, 1950.

Dawson, R. *The Present State of Australia*. London, 1831.

Delbridge, A. 'The Use of English in Australian Literature', *Harvard Educational Review*, vol. 34, 1963, no. 2. *See also* Mitchell, A. G.

Dennis, C. J. *Backblock Ballads and Other Verses*. Melbourne, 1913.

——— *Songs of a Sentimental Bloke*. Sydney, 1915.

——— *The Moods of Ginger Mick*. Sydney, 1916.

Dictionary of American English on Historical Principles, A, by W. A. Craigie and J. R. Hulbert. Chicago, 1938.

Dictionary of Americanisms on Historical Principles, A, by M. M. Mathews. Chicago, 1951.

Dictionary of the English Language, A, by Samuel Johnson. London, 1755.

Dictionary of Modern Slang, Cant, and Vulgar Words, A, by J. C. Hotten. 2nd ed. London, 1860.

Dictionary of Slang and Unconventional English, A, edited by E. Partridge. 4th ed. London, 1951.

Digger's Handbook and Truth about California, The, by D. L. Sydney, 1849.

Douglas, J. *Opportunity in Australia*. London, 1947.

Downing, W. H. *Digger Dialects*. Melbourne, 1919.

Dumaresq, W. J. *A Ride to Bathurst*, 1827 (ed. G. Mackaness). Australian Historical Monographs series. Sydney, 1950-1.

Eggleston, J., *see* Methodist Missionary Society, London.

Ehrensperger, C. 'Australianisms', *Taalstudie*, vol. 9. (Te Kuilenburg, 1888.)

English Dialect Dictionary, The, by Joseph Wright. London, 1898-1905.

Farmer, J. S., and Henley, W. E. *Dictionary of Slang and Colloquial English*. London, 1905.

Field, Barron. *Journal of an Excursion across the Blue Mountains*, 1822 (ed. G. Mackaness). Australian Historical Monographs series. Sydney, 1950.

Finch-Hatton, W. *Advance Australia: An Account of Eight Years' Work, Wandering and Amusement in Queensland, New South Wales and Victoria*. London, 1885.

Finger, C. J. *A Dog at his Heel*. London, 1937.

Fraser, J. (ed.). *An Australian Language*. Sydney, 1892.

Froude, J. A. *Oceana or England and her Colonies*. London, 1886.

Fullerton, M. E., *see Australian Comic Dictionary*.

Gamba, C. *The Italian Fishermen of Fremantle*. Perth, 1952.

Garth, J. W. 'Some Australian Slang', *Australian Magazine*, November 1908.

Gould, J. *Birds of Australia*. 7 vols. London, 1848.

Grant, W., and Murison, D. D. (ed.). *Scottish National Dictionary*. Edinburgh, 1931—.

Greenwood, G. *Early American-Australian Relations from the Arrival of the Spaniards in America to the close of 1830*. Melbourne, 1944.

Gregor, J. Journal, 1843. Society for the Propagation of the Gospel, London.

Grose, Francis. *A Classical Dictionary of the Vulgar Tongue*, 1796 text, edited by Eric Partridge. 3rd ed. London, 1963.

Gunther, J. 'Grammar and Vocabulary of the Aboriginal Dialect called the Wirradhuri', in J. Fraser, *An Australian Language*. Sydney, 1892.

———— Journal, 1836-40. Mitchell Library.

———— The Native Dialect Wirradurri, spoken in the Wellington District, etc. 1838. Mitchell Library.

Hancock, W. K. *Australia*. London, 1930.

Harris, Alexander. *Settlers and Convicts, or Recollections of Sixteen Years' Labour in the Australian Backwoods by an Emigrant Mechanic.* London, 1847; ed. C. M. H. Clark, Melbourne, 1953.

────── *The Emigrant Family, or the Story of an Australian Settler.* 3 vols. London, 1849.

Harrison, T. 'People: Wowsers', *New Statesman and Nation,* 23 November 1946.

Haskell, A. L. *Waltzing Matilda.* Sydney, 1940.

Hebart, T. *Die Vereinigte Evangelische Lutherische Kirche in Australien.* Adelaide, 1938.

Heysen, Hans. 'A German-Australian Village', *Lone Hand,* 1908.

Hetherington's Useful Handbook for Intending Emigrants. London, n.d.

Hicks, W. 'Australian Slang', *Life,* 18 April 1942.

Hight, J. *Manual of Derivation and Composition of Words.* New Zealand, n.d. [?1906].

Hill, Ernestine. *The Great Australian Loneliness.* Sydney, 1940.

Hodgson, C. P. *Reminiscences of Australia.* London, 1846.

Hotten, J. C. *A Dictionary of Modern Slang, Cant, and Vulgar Words.* 2nd ed. London, 1860.

Howitt, W. *Land, Labour and Gold, or Two Years in Victoria, with Visits to Sydney and Van Diemen's Land.* 2 vols. London, 1855.

Hunter, J. *An Historical Journal of the Transactions at Port Jackson and Norfolk Island, etc.* London, 1793.

Iredale, T., and Troughton, E. 'Captain Cook's Kangaroo', *Australian Zoologist,* 1925.

Jobson, F. J. *Australia.* London, 1862.

Johnson, Richard. *Some Letters of Rev. Richard Johnson* (ed. G. Mackaness). Australian Historical Monographs series. Sydney, 1955.

Johnson, Samuel. *A Dictionary of the English Language.* London, 1755.

Johnston, G. H. 'This War is Evolving New Army Slang', *Argus* (Melbourne), 15 November 1941.

Johnston, M. 'Aussie Dictionary', *Aussie,* 1918.

'Journal and Letters of Daniel Southwell, 1788-1792' (Southwell Papers), *H.R.N.S.W.*, vol. ii, Appendix D.

Jukes, J. B. (ed.). *Lectures on Gold for the Instruction of Emigrants about to Proceed to Australia.* London, 1852.

King, H. W. 'County, Shire and Town in New South Wales', *Australian Geographer* (1954), vol. vi, no. 3.

King, P. P. *Narrative of a Survey of the Intertropical and Western Coasts of Australia.* 2 vols. London, 1827.

Kingsley, H. *Recollections of Geoffrey Hamlyn.* London, 1859.

Krapp, G. P. *The English Language in America.* New York, 1925.

Lake, J. *A Dictionary of Australasian Words*, the Australasian Supplement to *Webster's International Dictionary.* Springfield, Mass., 1898.

Lancelott, F. *Australia As It Is, Its Settlements, Farms and Gold Fields.* 2 vols. London, 1852.

Lang, J. D. *Cooksland.* London, 1847.

Lawson, Henry. 'The Romance of the Swag', in *Prose Works of Henry Lawson.* Sydney, 1948.

Leigh, S., *see* Methodist Missionary Society, London.

Lentzner, Karl. 'Australisches Englisch', *Englische Studien* (1888), vol. xi.

—————— *Dictionary of the Slang-English of Australia and of Some Mixed Languages.* Halle-Leipzig, 1892.

Levi, W. *American-Australian Relations.* Minnesota, 1947.

Lhotsky, J. 'Some Remarks on a Short Vocabulary of the Natives of Van Diemen Land; and also of Menero Downs in Australia', *Royal Geographical Society of London Journal*, vol. 9, 1839.

Lodewyckx, A. *Die Deutschen in Australien.* Stuttgart, 1932.

Lyng, J. *Non-Britishers in Australia.* Melbourne, 1927.

—————— *The Scandinavians in Australia, New Zealand and the Western Pacific.* Melbourne, 1939.

McKnight, G. H. *English Words and Their Background.* New York, 1923.

McLachlan, N. (ed.). *The Memoirs of James Hardy Vaux.* London, 1964.

Macquarie, Lachlan. *Lachlan Macquarie, Governor of New South Wales: Journals of his Tours in New South Wales and Van Diemen's Land, 1810-22.* Sydney, 1956.

Madgwick, R. B. *Immigration into Eastern Australia.* London, 1937.

Mander, A. E. *The Making of the Australians.* London, 1958.

Marckwardt, A. H. *American English.* New York, 1958.

Marjoribanks, A. *Travels in New South Wales.* London, 1847.

Marshall, Vance, *see Timely Tips for New Australians.*

Mathew, J. *Eaglehawk and Crow.* Melbourne, 1899.

Mathews, M. M. *A Dictionary of Americanisms on Historical Principles.* Chicago, 1951.

Mathews, R. H. Collected Articles on the Languages of the Australian Aborigines (1901-10; Sydney Municipal Library).

Mencken, H. L. *The American Language.* New York, 1919; 4th ed., New York, 1962.

Methodist Missionary Society, London. Letters and Journals relating to Australia.

Mitchell, A. G. 'Australian English', *Australian Quarterly,* vol. XXIII, 1951, no 1.

——— 'Fighting Words', *Salt,* 22 December 1941.

——— 'Glossary of War Words', *Southerly,* no. 3, 1942.

——— *Supplement of Australian and New Zealand Words, Chambers's Shorter English Dictionary* (Aust. ed.). Sydney, 1952.

——— *The Pronunciation of English in Australia,* Sydney, 1946; rev. ed. by A. Delbridge, 1965.

——— *The Australian Accent.* Adelaide, 1961.

Mitchell, T. L. *Three Expeditions into the Interior of Eastern Australia.* 2 vols. London, 1838.

Moore, G. F. *A Descriptive Vocabulary of the Language in Common Use amongst the Aborigines of Western Australia.* London, 1842.

Moorehead, Alan. *Cooper's Creek.* London, 1963.

Morris, E. E. *Austral English, A Dictionary of Australasian Words, Phrases and Usages.* London, 1898.

Mossman, S., and Banister, T. *Australia Visited and Revisited*. London, 1853.

Mudie, James. *The Felonry of New South Wales* (1837) (ed. W. Stone). Melbourne, 1964.

Mundy, G. C. *Our Antipodes*. 3 vols. London, 1852.

New South Wales, Its Past, Present and Future Condition, by a Resident of Twelve Years' Experience. London, 1849.

Nind, S. 'Vocabulary of the Language of the Aborigines of Western Australia', *Royal Geographical Society of London Journal*, vol. 1, 1832; also in N. Ogle, *The Colony of Western Australia*. London, 1839.

O'Brien, S. E., and Stephens, A. G. Material for a Dictionary of Australian Slang. 1910. Mitchell Library.

O'Byrne, G. D. Reminiscences of my Three Voyages to Australia and Sixteen Years Experience as a Gold Miner on the Principal Fields of Victoria (1889-91). Rhodes House, Oxford.

Ogle, N. *The Colony of Western Australia*. London, 1839.

O'Meara, D. 'Australian "Cobber" ', *American Speech*, vol. 21, 1946, no. 4.

Oxford English Dictionary, The. Oxford, 1888-1928. *Supplement*, 1933.

Palmer, Nettie. 'Austral English', *Talking it Over*. Sydney, 1932.

Palmer, Vance. *The Legend of the Nineties*. Melbourne, 1954.

Partridge, Eric. *A Charm of Words*. London, 1960.

———— *A Dictionary of Slang and Unconventional English*. 4th ed. London, 1951.

———— 'Australian English', in *British and American English Since 1900* (ed. E. Partridge and J. W. Clark). London, 1951.

———— *Slang Today and Yesterday*. London, 1933.

———— 'Their Language', in *The Sunburnt Country* (ed. I. Bevan). London, 1953.

Partridge, E., and Clark, J. W. (ed.). *British and American English Since 1900*. London, 1951.

Paterson, G. *The History of New South Wales*. London, 1811.

'Paterson's Journal', *H.R.A.*, vol. III.

Pear, T. H. *Personality, Appearance and Speech.* London, 1957.

Pearl, Cyril. *Wild Men of Sydney.* London, 1958.

Pei, M. A. *The World's Chief Languages* (formerly *Languages for War and Peace*). London, 1949.

Penguin Book of Australian Ballads, edited by R. Ward. Melbourne, 1964.

Penguin Book of Australian Verse, edited by J. Thompson, K. Slessor, and R. G. Howarth. London, 1958.

Pettman, C. *Africanderisms.* London, 1913.

Price, C. A. *German Settlers in South Australia.* Melbourne, 1945.

———— *Southern Europeans in Australia.* Melbourne, 1963.

Pyke, N. P. O. 'Some Leading Aspects of Foreign Immigration to the Goldfields', *Royal Australian Historical Society Journal and Proceedings,* vol. 33, 1947, pt 1.

Quinn, J. 'Diggers Add to the Dictionary', *Sun* (Sydney), 26 August 1942.

Ramson, W. S. *The Currency of Aboriginal Words in Australian English.* Occasional Research Paper No. 3, Australian Language Research Centre. Sydney, 1964.

Read, C. R. *What I Heard, Saw, and Did at the Australian Gold Fields.* London, 1853.

Redford, Arthur. *Labour Migration in England, 1800-1850.* Manchester, 1926.

Ridley, W. *Kamilaroi, Dippil and Turrubul.* Sydney, 1866.

———— *Kamilaroi and other Australian Languages.* Sydney, 1875.

Roberts, S. H. *The Squatting Age in Australia, 1835-1847.* Melbourne, 1935.

Robson, L. L. *The Convict Settlers of Australia.* Melbourne, 1965.

Roth, H. L. *The Aborigines of Tasmania.* Halifax, U.K., 1899.

Rowcroft, Charles. *The Bushranger of Van Diemen's Land.* 3 vols. London, 1843.

Russell, A. *A Tour Through The Australian Colonies in 1839.* London, 1840.

Rutter, S. *Hints to Gold Hunters.* Sydney, 1851.

Sayers, E. S. *Pidgin English.* Toronto, 1939.

Schonell, F. J., Meddleton, I. G., and Shaw, B. A. *A Study of the Oral Vocabulary of Adults.* Brisbane, 1956.

Schuchardt, H. 'Beiträge zur kenntnis des englischen Kreolisch', *Englische Studien*, vol. xii, 1889, vol. xiii, 1890.

Scottish National Dictionary, ed. W. Grant and D. D. Murison. Edinburgh, [1931—   ].

Serle, G. *The Golden Age.* Melbourne, 1963.

Sharwood, J., and Gerson, S. 'The Vocabulary of Australian English', *Moderna Språk*, vol. lvii, 1963.

Simonini, R. C., Jr. 'Etymological Categories of Present-Day English and their Productivity', *Language Learning*, vol. 9, 1959, no. 1.

'Slang Down Under', *New York Times Magazine.* 7 January 1943.

Smyth, R. B. *The Aborigines of Victoria.* 2 vols. London, 1878.

——— *The Goldfields and Mineral Districts of Victoria.* Melbourne, 1869.

Southwell Papers, *see* 'Journal and Letters of Daniel Southwell'.

Stevans, C. M. (ed.). *The World's Standard Dictionary.* Rev. ed. Auckland, N.Z., 1915.

Stewart, Douglas, and Keesing, Nancy (ed.). *Old Bush Songs and Rhymes of Colonial Times.* Sydney, 1957.

Strong, H. A. 'Austral English and Slang', *University Extension Journal* (London), vol. 3, 1898, no. 23.

Sturt, C. Journal from May 22nd to June 20th, 1838. Rhodes House, Oxford.

Sturt, J. M. 'Diary'. Rhodes House, Oxford.

Sydney Slang Dictionary, The. Sydney, [1882?].

Taplin, G. *The Narinyeri.* Adelaide, 1878.

Teichelmann, C. G., and Schuermann, C. W. *Outline of a Grammar, Vocabulary, and Phraseology of the Aboriginal Language of South Australia.* Adelaide, 1840.

Tench, Watkin. *A Complete Account of the Settlement at Port Jackson in New South Wales.* London, 1793.

Thatcher, Charles. 'The Green New-Chum', in Douglas Stewart and Nancy Keesing (ed.). *Old Bush Songs and Rhymes of Colonial Times*. Sydney, 1957.

Thompson, G. *Slavery and Famine, Punishment for Sedition*, 1794 (ed. G. Mackaness). Australian Historical Monographs series. Sydney, 1947.

Thomson, A. K. 'Australian English', in *British and American English since 1900* (ed. E. Partridge and J. W. Clark). London, 1951.

Threlkeld, L. E. *An Australian Grammar*. Sydney, 1834.

—— Papers. Mitchell Library.

Timely Tips for New Australians, by 'Jice Doone' (Vance Marshall). London, 1926.

Tipsmill, George. 'The Snake', in Douglas Stewart and Nancy Keesing (ed.), *Old Bush Songs*.

Tucker, S. *English Examined*. Cambridge, 1961.

Tuckfield, F., *see* Methodist Missionary Society, London.

Twopeny, R. E. N. *Town Life in Australia*. London, 1883.

Vaux, James Hardy. *A New and Comprehensive Vocabulary of the Flash Language* (1819), in *The Memoirs of James Hardy Vaux* (1819) (ed. N. McLachlan). London, 1964.

Wakefield, E. G. *A Letter from Sydney*. London, 1829; Everyman ed., 1929.

Walker, D. *We Went to Australia*. London, 1949.

Walker, W., *see* Methodist Missionary Society, London.

Ward, Russel. *The Australian Legend*. Melbourne, 1958.

Watling, T. *Letters from an Exile at Botany Bay* (ed. G. Mackaness). Australian Historical Monographs series. Sydney, 1945.

Watson, W. Letters, Journal and Reports, 1832-42. Church Missionary Society, London.

Webster's New International Dictionary of the English Language. Springfield, Mass., 1961.

Wells, T. E. *Michael Howe, The Last and Worst of the Bushrangers of the Van Diemen's Land* (ed. G. Mackaness). Australian Historical Monographs series. Sydney, 1945.

Westgarth, W. *Australia Felix*. London, 1848.

White, J. *A Journal of a Voyage to New South Wales.* London, 1790.

Wierzbicki, —. *Guide to the Gold Regions*; Appendix to E. Bryant, *What I Saw in California.* Launceston, 1850.

Wood, Thomas. *Cobbers.* London, 1934.

World's Standard Dictionary, The (ed. C. M. Stevans). Rev. ed. Auckland, N.Z., 1915.

Wright, Joseph. *The English Dialect Dictionary.* London, 1898-1905.

Index to Words and Phrases

N

General Index

General Index